YOU ARE MY FATHER

I AM YOUR SON

BY
Dr. Kelafo Z. Collie, MD
Foreword by Dr. Myles Munroe

Published by:
Majestic Priesthood Publication, Freeport, Grand
Bahama, Bahamas.
Email: mpppublications@gmail.com
s1-242-559-2138

Romans 8:12-24"Therefore, brothers, we have an obligation—but it is not to the sinful nature, to live according to it. [13] For if you live according to the sinful nature, you will die; but if by the Spirit you put to death the misdeeds of the body, you will live, [14] **because those who are led by the Spirit of God are sons of God. [15] For you did not receive a spirit that makes you a slave again to fear, but you received the Spirit of sonship. And by him we cry,** *"Abba,* **Father."** [16] The Spirit himself testifies with our spirit that we are God's children. [17] Now if we are children, then we are heirs—heirs of God and co-heirs with Christ, if indeed we share in his sufferings in order that we may also share in his glory.[18]I consider that our present sufferings are not worth comparing with the glory that will be revealed in us. [19] **The creation waits in eager expectation for the sons of God to be revealed.** [20] For the creation was subjected to frustration, not by its own choice, but by the will of the one who subjected it, in hope [21] that the creation itself will be liberated from its bondage to decay and brought into the glorious freedom of the children of God. [22] We know that the whole creation has been groaning as in the pains of childbirth right up to the present time. [23] Not only so, but we ourselves, who have the first fruits of the Spirit, groan inwardly as we wait eagerly for our adoption as sons, the redemption of our bodies.

John 1:11"He came unto his own, and his own received him not. [12]But as many as received him, to them gave he power to become the sons of God, *even* to them that believe on his name: [13]Which were born, not of blood, nor of the will of the flesh, nor of the will of man, but of God."

Table of Contents

"The Father's Voice"

You are my son; today I have begotten you, You call me Father, and I hear your cry, For they which are led by the Spirit, To them are the sons of God.

You are my Son; I am your Father, All I have, I give unto thee.

You are my son, I am your Father. Even if you've fallen, come unto me. Inside my mind I have a plan for you,

No man has seen or heard what I have prepared.

I know your needs before you ask,

I love you still, in spite of your past.

Listen to my voice and I will give the inheritance to you,

Grow in my word and direct your path.

I will watch over you in the midnight hour.

With my Spirit, I have raised you with power.

(Reference **Psalm 2:7**)

Written By Dr. Kelafo Z. Collie MD

Dedications

(Understanding Sonship Authority)

"I will declare the decree: the Lord hath said unto me, Thou art my Son; this day have I begotten thee." Vs. 8 "Ask of me, and I shall give thee the heathen for thine inheritance, and the utter-most parts of the earth for thy possession." Vs 9 "Thou shalt break them with a rod of iron; thou shalt dash them in pieces like a potter's vessel."

Psalms 2:7

This book is dedicated to Jehovah, my heavenly Father, who has called me His 'Son' through Christ Jesus and has made me apart of His family. As a 'Son' I have stepped into an understanding of a loving Father who longs for fellowship with me and has given me His nature.

I extend special dedications to my biological father, Bishop Sidney Collie who has been a mentor and inspirational dad to his children. It was through his fatherhood that I was better able to understand true father-son relationships and was able to parallel it to my heavenly Father.

To my Spiritual covering and mentors, Bishop James Rodney Roberts of Five Porches of Deliverance Apostolic Tabernacle and Apostle Bertril Baird of Trinidad. Thank you for mentoring and releasing me into Church Ministry to equip the saints. To all Spiritual Leaders whose ministry and message have impacted my life including: Dr. Myles Munroe, the late Apostle Turnel Nelson, Pastor Samuel Phillips and Bishop Ross Davis, thank you for releasing many into purpose and Sonship.

To every human across the world whose life has been broken and limited because they did not understand their position, relationship and authority in Christ. This book is an attempt to restore man's true identity in Jesus.

Finally, this book was inspired to teach and encourage you to be all that God called you to be and achieve; to stand as a whole person.

I extend special dedications to children born of single parents, rape, broken marriage and adoptions.

To the nations in whom children are being born in oppressed societies, with broken self-confidence and shattered dreams because of opinions and limited resources.

This message is for you!!

FOREWORD

*T*his erudite, eloquent, and immensely thought-provoking work gets to the heart of the deepest contradictions within our culture; the need for understanding the Kingdom of God and its relation to our daily lives.

This is indispensable reading for anyone who wants to live life above the norm. This is a profound authoritative work which spans the wisdom of the ages and yet breaks new ground in its approach and will possibly become a classic in this and the next generation.

This exceptional work by Dr. Kelafo Z. Collie is one of the most profound, practical, principle-centered approaches to this subject of the Kingdom I have read in a long time. The author's approach to this timely issue brings a fresh breath of air that captivates the heart, engages the mind and inspires the spirit of the reader.

The author's ability to leap over complicated theological and metaphysical jargon and reduce complex theories to simple practical principles that the least among us can understand is amazing. This work will challenge the intellectual while embracing the laymen as it dismantles the mystery of the soul search of mankind and delivers the profound in simplicity.

Dr. Kelafo's approach awakens in the reader the untapped inhibiters that retard our personal development and his anti-dotes empower us to rise above these self-defeating, self-limiting factors to a life of exploits in spiritual and mental advancement. He brings the Kingdom alive.

The author also integrates into each chapter the time-tested precepts of the Kingdom, giving each principle a practical application to life making the entire process people-friendly.

Every sentence of this book is pregnant with wisdom, and I enjoyed the mind-expanding experience of this exciting book. I admonish you to plunge into this ocean of knowledge and watch your life change for the better as you accept the truth that God is your father and you are his son.

Dr. Myles Munroe
Bahamas Faith Ministries International
ITWLA
Nassau Bahamas

PREFACE

*W*e are at the dawn of what I have coined the greatest period of mankind, an era of technological and medical breakthroughs, yet the quest for self-awareness remains unanswered.

Humans are thriving in the heartbeat of the greatest era of advancement for mankind. This piece of the millennium has exposed humans to technological innovations, medical discoveries even social and racial integration. Yet in the soul of men across every race, culture, socio-economic position and nationality lies a quest for self-awareness and dominion over life.

Questions are reverberating throughout the globe about world-wide peace in the midst of national and personal turmoil. Many are earnestly searching for security distinct from an uncertain and highly volatile financial market.

Most noticeably, the creature known as man (mankind) is ripe for spiritual truths. Their hearts lay moist, soil waiting for seeds to be implanted to take root and grow to the full awareness of God. From the delinquent to the distinguished, man wants to know about the God who will somehow put into perspective the purpose for which they existence. Maybe you feel that life is a cycle of events that seem to just crash into oblivion; need a sense of divine destiny and purpose.

Transcending all ethnic, cultures, financial status and nationalities, men are scanning for groups of people who exemplify peace in the midst of personal and national turmoil; financial stability in an uncertain and volatile financial market. Most emphatically, man is searching for truths in a creator, a God who will somehow put into perspective the purpose of life in which so many wonder aimlessly from day to day.

There is someone reading this book who feels stuck in a ritual of events that seem to go nowhere. You feel that your wholeness lies in financial success; to your dismay, you achieve great financial wealth but still feel empty on the inside of your soul.

Hence, you scramble to love and happiness with a lover and readily find out that it is only taking leading you down a lonely road of darkness. You now wonder if this is the only experience of life, a road of ups and downs and treacherous turns…

The book of **John 10:10** *"The thief cometh not, but for to steal, and to kill and to destroy:*

I am come that they might have life and they might have more abundantly."

The word translated '*life*' in that verse is the Greek word 'Zoë'. It means the "God-kind of life." It's the abundant, victorious life; you can experience right here in this world when the anointing of God is in you and upon you. The anointing is the supernatural wisdom and strength to live a victorious life! In the following verses, one can see how this anointing brings you supernatural understanding and knowledge to win.

I John 2:26-27 *"These things have I written unto you concerning them that seduce you. But the anointing which ye have receive of Him abided in you, and ye need not that any man teach you: but as the same anointing teacheth you all things and is truth, and is no lie, and even as it hath taught you, ye shall abide in Him."*

Do you know why many are not achieving that purpose? One may have been continuously struggling with lust, homosexuality, depression and the scars of broken relationships. The fact is if you are overcome with any of these things, you are not living the Zoë life. (Zoë according to the *Lexical Aids* to the New Testament means 'life,' the principle of life in the Spirit and Soul.) Zoë is a word that details a nobler royal life. It expresses all of the highest standards and best of which Christ has is offer, and that which He gives to the believer. It is the highest blessings and excellence of the creator God.

Jesus says in **John 6:33** (NIV), *"The Spirit gives life; the flesh counts for nothing. The words that I have spoken to you they are spirit and they are life."* Sadly, many today teach only how to be good members who serve in every capacity of their church, from paying tithes to preaching, yet sons and daughters of the Lord are chained to sin and defeat.

The challenge is many of our churches have taught only to live a portion of the total authority given to us through a Spirit-filled life.

There are untapped dimensions of life found not by being a member of the church only but by being a citizen of the Kingdom of God. As you are filled with the logos word of this book, the spirit of the Lord will speak to your situation and transform your destiny!!!!

It might be that your deepest desire for living is to gain solely financial success, and your life outside of monetary security is unthinkable. However, in the midst of great wealth and material possession, life is still chaotic, unfulfilling and inside your soul secretly lays a lonely, unhappy, miserable child. As an alternative to wealth, many scramble to find self-fulfillment and happiness in a love relationship; this decision sometimes rapidly lead down a road of emotional pain, broken promises and lost dreams. The point can be argued if this unpredictable cycle of events called life has any consistency to it? Or is it a road of ups, down and treacherous turns…

I am convinced that there is a pattern for this life that brings strength, energy and a victorious life. Every individual can take control and bring clarity to all areas concerning their life.

Firstly, there are a few guidelines to taking control of life and preventing daily circumstances accumulating in life long frustration understands spiritual principles. The spiritual principles reference is the Bible, which is the infallible, inerrant word and instruction of God to mankind. The Bible references that are presented in this book will open the solutions to overcoming this world while living in it. The scriptures will give instruction in transforming the thoughts of defeated weak individuals into an overcoming, powerful dominating human you were created to be.

In the preceding chapters, the locks will be opened to the steps of a spectacular level of human existence. Your life will never be the same and the will of God will be illuminated and revitalized in your life in Jesus' name.

Sons will be birthed through the affirmation in the name of Jesus. The 'name' generally specifies the character of an individual. Name carries with it the authority of that individual the credibility of the life of the person.

The name of Jesus carries tremendous authority in the natural and spiritual realms. *"At the name of Jesus every knee shall bow and every tongue confess that He is owner of everything."* His name also provides access to the father; it is the only name whereby mankind can be salvaged and restored to sonship. It is through the name, authority credibility and influence of Jesus that sons are born in the Spirit. The sons can be born in the will of the father Praise God!!!!

The word 'son' is not a term of gender but one of relationship. It indicates a position of fellowship with God. These qualities lead to the maturing of a churchgoer to that of a believer with access and authority to conduct the will of God in the Earth. This position of Sonship crosses all manmade barriers. It slices through the ethnic, racial and socioeconomic barriers that would have marginalize the believer from walking in their God given authority. Sonship has unlimited potential to propel a believer into every promise and blessing that their heavenly Father has in store for us.

Romans 8:14 "For as many as are led by the spirit of God, they are the sons of God."

The Kingdom of Sons Mission Declarations:

The Vision of the Father's sonship plan:

*T*o establish a nation of Sons under the King Jesus who demonstrates the glory of Christ Jesus' love, character, righteousness and mighty power.

The Father's Kingdom purpose of sonship:

The Father desires to reintroduce Himself as the Creator of heaven, earth and all human life. He desires the restoration of mankind in the understanding of their sonship potential and inheritance as spiritually matured individuals in the earth; hence placing all of creation under the dominion ruler-ship and nature of the King Jesus Christ.

The Holy Spirit who is the person of Jesus will live inside the sons' thus ruling and reigning first through the believer and then impacting the earth with His righteous character.

Chapter 1

"Meet the Parent, introducing the Father"

!"

Psalms 89:26 "He shall cry unto me, thou art my father, my God, and the rock of my salvation."

Psalms 2:7 "I will declare the decree: the Lord hath said unto me, Thou art my Son; this day have I begotten thee."

Psalms 2:8 "Ask of me, and I shall give thee the heathen for thine inheritance, and the uttermost parts of the earth for thy possession."

Psalm 2:9 "Thou shalt break them with a rod of iron; thou shalt dash them in pieces like a potter's vessel."

*T*he artistic songwriter and King David who rose to prom-inence as the mighty, skilled, militant leader over Israel from the meadows of sheep rearing met the Father creator. David assisted in the conquering of many territories for his nation and established one of the greatest historic empires; introduces the world to the Father who is God. The reference of God is made to the deity that revealed Himself through nature and the elements but also to the people of Israel. This God is the Father as seen in the Bible and will later be noted to walk on earth as the person of Jesus Christ.

King David through very extreme situations of warfare, treason and betrayal began to seek out diligently this Father God and creator of life. This Father was known by David's ancestors and forefathers by His supernatural miracles but also by tangible ways of physically appearing, speaking to, providing and protecting this nation of nomadic people.

Interestingly, David in the first stanza of the text not only alludes to this deity being a God but a Father to him. Although embedded in these words written by David were prophetic declarations of the Messiah Jesus Christ (The Anointed King) to come; we have a pathway to meet this God and Father.

This intriguing point leaped out from this text as most philosophies, doctrines and religions of the earth historically ascribe only dread and fear of their deities. What was different about this God that David met?

How was it that he (David) could so comfortable designating this most powerful, supreme, immortal being as a Father?

As I reflect on those precious moments with my biological father, the times of learning and exchange I parallel it to understanding this eternal father. There were seasons of sharing about life and events that arose from time to time. He delicately engraved life's lessons into my mind and heart that are irreplaceable. I could not help but parallel this natural relationship with the Father who is God. My biological father cheered me as I moved in the right direction and sharply corrected me when I was about to make very poor decisions. Occasionally, he took time to train and prepare me for the future just like my heavenly Father did.

These acts so reflect the love and express nature of the heavenly Father. He gently gives us His words for success, tenderly corrects us and pleads for us to come back to Him after we have ignorantly wondered away.

The mental picture that develops immediately when the term, 'father' is mentioned is a person of whom a one is born or offspring from. The imprint on my mind is the picture of a strong man with order and honour in the family. He is one with direction, courage and vigorously defends the home. A father can be perceived as one who works diligently to provide all of the resources of food, shelter, clothing and financial provision. He is strong leader with his wisdom and discipline; however warm and gently to soothe the childlike fears and doubts that sometimes overwhelm the heart of an innocent child. A loving father lives for the fulfilment of dreams and success of his offspring.

This reminds me of an imaginary scene in an over-crowded shopping mall one Christmas season a young female child stood in the centre crying intensely with her head hang down. Many swarmed around her including the police who dishearten was not able to console the distress of this child. As I drew closer from a distance into this commotion, I soon realized that this child was accidentally left by her parents; perhaps through the flashing crowds, she was misplaced. As I looked on her face; it was crimson red, her eyes were flooded with tears that rolled down her cheeks and onto the floor.

The ice-cream cone she aimlessly held drained down her hands splashed onto the floors as though she had completely abandoned it to the elements.

Suddenly, from the behind crowds resound a loud thunderous cry "Karen, Karen," it seems to have echoed throughout the entire mall. In midst of the sounds of Christmas, the little girl looked up with overwhelming anticipation, in the direction of the voice. Without delay she began to squeeze through the

4

layers of onlookers, peeling them back as she passionately reached towards the voice.

As she pushed through the people who encircle her, light shone towards her and she saw a tall, muscular male figure that cried again this time in a caring overtone "Karen darling where have you been?" The child instantly dropped the ice-cream cone and began to dash towards the man almost melodiously singing "Daddy, Daddy, Daddy!" and sprung into his arms and he embraced her. My thoughts flashed to the Psalms of David, as I watched that child confidently hang from her father's arms. Her face shone brightly; all of her fears were gone. David emphatically began to share inti-mate similarities about this God being like this loving father portrayed in this story.

This text began to clarify not simply a disconnected God but an intimate father to son relation. Could this be blasphemous at the core for mortal men to ascribe such intimate contact with immortality? Is it unimaginable to also declare that He (Deity) is Father to all beings?

This passage sparked my curiosity and is sure it is over-flowing the glasses of your minds now. Let us examine carefully the meanings of the words in the quotations. If there is truly a God who is all-powerful and He is my Father then I need to meet true family and identity, how about you?

The word "Father" according to the *Vine's Complete Expository Dictionary* is denoted as '***Ab*' or '*Abba*'** in the Hebraic language. It refers to or relates to the familial relationship represented by the word 'Father'. It may be used of anyone of the entire lineage of men from whom a given individual is descended. It described God as one who begot and protects. He must always be revered and obeyed. It can also refer to the following:

- A forefather, including a clan, a special group of leaders.
- A dynasty or nation of people.
- It can describe the adoptive relationships of one person to another.
- It alludes to a title of respect.

The New Testament Greek translates the word Father as 'Pater' (3962- *Vine's Complete Expository Dictionary*) which from a root word denotes:

- The God as the Father of lights. He is the source or giver of illuminations, physical and spiritual.
- God as the creator of the universe.
- A nourisher, protector, upholder of His people and creation.

Lexical Aids to the New Testament denotes:

"Progenitor

- ✎ One who resembles another in disposition, actions as children usually do their parents; an author or initi-ator of anything.
- ✎ This term speaks of God, denoting His divine nature and essence as Father of man creation."

The book of Hebrew **12:9** states *"Furthermore we have had fathers of our flesh which corrected us, and gave them reverence: shall we not much rather is in subjection unto the Father of spirits live?"*

The inference from the Psalms portray that David who is a man is a Son of the deity. To be a father means first (Source) DNA or genetic code of one individual is replicated in the DNA of another being (offspring). It means that that offspring carries the material that is most exactly identical to its source. The offspring now develops the same characteristics, nature, species, name and identity of the parent. The offspring reproduces in order to continue the survival of that species while maintaining the integrity, character and identity of the original source (Father). Therefore, our future meaning of life and our true essence lie in earnestly finding out who this God of the Bible is; who wants to hold us in His arms and speak words of life into our ears. Let's get ready to meet Him, our Father!!!

Chapter 1 End of Chapter - Principles:

- Jehovah God is our heavenly Father who walked the earth as Jesus Christ.

- A father is one with order and honour in the family.

- Father is one with direction, courage and defends the home.

- Father is the source; of life, shelter, clothing and financial provision.

- Father is denoted Ab or Abba in the Hebrews.

- Abba means: - A forefather, source and a title of respect. Greek term is 'Pater' Source, or Giver or of provider of physical and spiritual in life. Also a nourisher and protector.

- Offspring of the Father (Heavenly) should possess the same characteristic nature and identity of the Father (Source).

Chapter 2

The Father's name
and character

!"

*I*t is inconceivable to imagine articulating words to such a great and majestic God our Father. He is the God and supreme ruler of the Bible. He is immensely far beyond the scope of our finite imaginations. He has done mighty acts and deeds throughout time. He is able to number all the hairs on every individual's heads while watching a sparrow fall to the ground. He can hear all of the requests of those who cry out to Him and respond to them all simultaneously. With His voice, He created the heavens and the earth and with His hands, He formed the first man. Yet scientific research in all of its advance high-tech instruments has not been able to form man from the dust particles and restore life to one that has died.

However, the Bible records certain aspects of the nature of this Father who revealed Himself and His character names to many persons.

The *Vine's Complete Expository Dictionary* denotes that 'name' in which God in the Hebrew (Old Testament) signifies. Here are the following examples:

∀ Seem (8034) – "name, reputation; memory" – To clarify this point the name often signifies or illuminates the essence of an individual.

∀ The names by which God revealed Himself describe something of His person and work.

The New Testament translation in the *Vine's Complete Expository Dictionary* denotes 'name' as the following:

'Onoma' (3686) - In general of the 'name' by which a person or thing is called.

Aname implies, of authority, character, rank, majesty, power, excellence.

The name of God as expressing His attributes.

We, therefore, can infer that name used by God the Father to His people throughout the Bible expresses a snapshot of His character based on the dominant attributes He exhibited to the nation of Israel at various points in time.

In **Psalms 68:4-5** the songwriter expresses emphatically:

"Sing unto God, praise to His name: extol Him that rideth upon the heavens by His name JAH, and rejoice before Him. A father of the fatherless, and a judge of the widows, is God in His holy habitation."

Here we see the names of the God of the Bible relaying and expresses His nature as JAH. Remember this is not the full character of God in like manner; one cannot summarize the dimensions of length and depth of any human life. One may be a son who is a student and also a musician but at a musical concert the dominant expression of that individual while skilfully playing the piano will be that of a musician.

However, there is tremendous deep and understanding in the name 'JAH' which assist in knowing this Father.

Lexical Aids to the Old Testament denotes *'JAH' (3050) or 'YAH'* which is a contracted formed of *'Yehowah'* (3063). This expresses His divine title. *'Yehowah'-* is Lord most vehement; powerful.

Jehovah is translated 'Lord' 6347 times. *Jehovah or Yehowah* is the self-existent or eternal one who keeps cove-nant and fulfill promises."

'Yah' is used in conjunction with *'Yehowah'* in **Isaiah 12:2** *"Behold, God is my salvation; I will trust and not be afraid: for the Lord Jehovah is my strength and my song; He also is become my salvation."*

Isaiah 26:4 *"Trust ye in the Lord forever: for in the Lord Jehovah is everlasting strength:"*

The term *Lord* (3068) used by *Lexical Aids* to the Old Testament denotes *Yehowah*, the covenant name of God most prominently known in connection with His relationship with the nation of Israel. It was never spoken by the Jews because of the reverence to the name. They hence substituted it with *'adonay 'elohim'* which means *"The Lord God."*

'Elohim' is translated as God, Living, Holy, Righteous, and True.

Vine's Complete Expository Dictionary denotes 'Adonay' as:

∀ The Lord over all, master which signifies "possessor" or "owner".

∀ When applied to God it signifies His position as the one who has authority (like) a master over His own people.

∀ One who is sovereign ruler and almighty master, a title of respect.

It is becoming clear that this Jehovah God is indeed an awesome and powerful being. He is the owner of everything in the heavens, the earth, the seas and all that existence. This is inclusive of every human. He is the sovereign owner and master. He is a Father who is faithful to promises and cove-nant towards His children who accept and trust Him through Jesus Christ.

Here are but a few titles used to grasp a glimpse of this Father of ours.

✄ Jehovah Elohim – It means the Self-Existent or Eternal Creator, the Elohim in covenant relationship with His people. The immutable One (not capable of or susceptible to change).

✄ Adonai – Jehovah – The Lord our sovereign; Master Jehovah.

✄ Jehovah Jireh – The Lord will see or provide

✄ Jehovah Nissi – The Lord our banner

✄ Jehovah Ropheka – The Lord our healer

✄ Jehovah Shalom – The Lord our Peace.

✄ Jehovah Tsidkeenu – The Lord our Righteousness.

- Jehovah Mekaddisskem – The Lord our sanctifier.
- Jehovah – Saboth – The Lord of Host.
- Jehovah Shammah – The Lord is present.
- Jehovah Elyon – The Lord most High.
- Jehovah Rohi – The Lord my Shepherd.
- Jehovah Eloheenu – The Lord our God.
- Jehovah Eloheka – The Lord thy God.
- Jehovah – Elohay – The Lord my God.
- El Elyon – Highest sovereign of the Heavens and the earth.
- Hasadiah – Jehovah is kind.
- Hashabnah – Jehovah is a friend.
- Jehoshua – Jehovah is salvation

What an amazing list of qualities for a great God and Father. It is very reassuring to know that our heavenly Father is much more than a great God sitting on a golden throne in Heaven. On the contrary, He is one that will provide all of the needs of His people according to His riches in glory for His purposes. His provision is infinite because He is the sovereign inherent owner of everything. This means not by inheritance or by transference but it is originally and solely His own property. Imagine a father that can also give peace. Peace is 'the state of being of rest and strong tranquility regardless of the changing environments.' The Father can give a sustaining reassure to the fears of all His people that all things will work out to the benefit of those who trust on His nature as a Father of peace. He will give comfort in the midst of the global recession and financial instability.

Consider a cancer-ridden individual believing that their body can be completely healed just by asking their Heavenly Father to do so. Jesus declared that there is no good thing the Father withhold from them that walk in right relationship with the Father.

These descriptions are even more powerful than any natural, biological father can even imagine being capable of doing. Visualize this Heavenly Father being able to sanctify His children. This simply means that this Father has the capacity and desire to remove all the debris of deep hurts, addictions and rebellion to His words. He can set His children apart from everyone for a special purpose and destiny. He would make His children very successful in His purposes for them.

In the midst of a world that is filled with terrorism, warfare, emergence of cure-less diseases, economic hardship and senseless murder of unborn children; it is comforting to know that the Father is "Hasadiah" – Jehovah is kind. His desires and heart is favourable towards His children. His thoughts are excellent towards His children; they are thoughts to prosper, bless and to lead His children to an end point that is bountiful, bliss and blessed.

The titles get even better with the name *"Jehoshua"* (English- Joshua) – meaning *"Jehovah Saves."* or *"Jehovah Saves."* Interestingly, this title transliterated in the New Testament Greek is the name *Jesus;* God saves or Saviour. This point will be explored more throughout this book as Jesus Christ of Nazareth's claim of being one with this Eternal God and Father Jehovah. It will be demonstrated through Jesus as His character and nature as He walked in the earth 2,000 years ago.

Chapter 2 End of Chapter Principles

∀ The term 'name' signifies 'seem' – name, reputation and memory. It also implies authority, character, rank, majesty, power and excellence.

∀ Name of God express His attributes.

∀ The name of God as seen in The Old Testament is 'JAH' or 'YAH' – contracted formed of 'Yehowah'.

∀ Yehowah or Jehovah means the 'self-existent' or 'eternal one' Yehowah is also denoted as 'Lord'.

∀ 'Lord' is also translated 'Adonay' meaning 'Lord over all or master' which signifies "possessor" or 'owner'.

∀ Jehovah revealed His character and nature to His people in many ways throughout history hence His many titles.

∀ Jehovah walked the earth and was named 'Jesus'.

∀ Jehovah wants to be an intimate loving friend, advisor protector and encourager to all humanity.

Chapter 3

The Father's Nature

!"

II Corinthians 3:17 "Now the Lord
is that Spirit: and where the Spirit
of the Lord is, there is liberty."

Hebrews 12: 9 "Furthermore we
have had fathers of our flesh
which corrected us, and we gave
them reverence: shall we not
much rather be in subjection unto
the Father of spirits and live?"

I John 5:7 "For these three that
bear record in heaven, the Father,
the Word and the Holy Spirit: and
these three are one."

*T*he above scriptural text gives a description of the God our Father. The Lord Jehovah is a spiritual being. This concept must be expounded on for the empirically evidence-based minds.

Lexical Aids to the New Testament translates the word "Spirit" to PNEUMA (4151) **1.** This relates to the invisible, immaterial and powerful. It is parallel to the wind. This expresses the character of the person of Jehovah.

2. It also denotes the breath of man; the element by which man perceives, reflects, feels, desires the invisible, immaterial part of man.

Father Jehovah is not difficult to understand because He is invisible, the elements of nature such as the wind prove that not invisible object do exist. Medical science can very easily verify these remarks as there are trillions of microscopic organisms that live on one's skin. They are not seen with the naked eye but are very viable and real.

Then there are very tiny non-living particles like protons, neutrons, and electrons that make up the basic structure of many of the elements in chemicals and even electricity.

God the Father exists and is very real and can be proven empirically. Here the text alludes to Jehovah being the father or source of all Spirits. He is the material from which every spiritual being is derived and He has the capacities to protect, provide for and nurture all beings. **John 4:24** *"God is a spirit and they that worship Him must worship Him in Spirit and in Truth."*

Most interestingly, we now examine the diversity and trichotomy of Jehovah God. John writes that there are three in heaven, namely the Father, whom we have hopefully been introduced to, and now the other two members.

Ladies and Gentlemen, I introduce to some and reac-quaint to others; the Most Holy and honourable person of the Father, The Word (Jesus the Christ) and the Holy Spirit.

Interestingly we see in the Book of **I John 5:7** *"For there are three that bear record in heaven, the Father, the Word, and the Holy Ghost: and these three are one."* **John 4:24** *"God is a Spirit and they that worship Him must worship Him in spirit and truth."*

> **I Chronicles 17:13** *"I will be His father, and He shall be my son: I will not take my mercy away from him, as I took it from Him that was before thee."* **(vs.14)** *"But I will settle Him in mine house and in my*

kingdom forever: and His throne shall be established forevermore."

II Samuel 7:14 *"I will be His father, and He shall be my son. If He commits iniquity, I will chasten Him with the rods of men, and with the stripes of the chil-dren of men:"*

Psalm 68:5 *"A father of the fatherless, and a judge of widows, is God in His holy habitation."*

A loving Father that knows your needs.

(He gives good and perfect gifts)

Matthew 6:7 – *"But when ye pray, use not vain repetitions as the heathen do: for they think that they shall be heard for their much speaking."*

Matthew 6:8 – *"Be not ye therefore like unto them: for your Father knoweth what things ye have need of before ye ask Him."*

Jesus is teaching with profound truth the mysteries of Kingdom living and culture. He is expounding on not praying in vain loud words of repetition in front of others to be seen and praised. It was common for spiritual leaders of biblical time and our time to say long prayers with eloquent words but had distorted motives. It was not for communicating and petitioning before the Lord but for the applause of men.

Jesus warns us not to be like them, but the sons of God must be always aware that our Heavenly Father knows our needs. This includes financial needs and obligations, the desires of our heart to see our loved ones saved or even to accomplish through Christ the destiny and visions God has placed in us. He knows that we need the resources to succeed, just relax and wait until he speaks to your hearts about the instruction to receive the needs. He wants total dependency on His word and Holy Spirit for His children to tap into the resources of the Kingdom wealth for every need. In fact, He does not want an occasional blessing to trickle on the needs of His children. He wants a wellspring of His anointing, streams of wisdom and secret treasures of hidden places to overflow the deserts of His Sons lives. Hallelujah unto our Lord and Father!

What an amazingly caring and considered Father we have. We are always on His mind; we are the love of His life and His prized possession. There is nothing He does not want to do for His precious and obedient children. The song-writer David describes in His words in the Book of

Psalms 8 (vs. 3) *"When I consider thy heavens, the work of thy fingers, the moon and the stars, which thou hast ordained;***(vs. 4)** *What is man that thou art mindful of him*

and the son of man that thou visit Him? **(vs. 5)** *For thou hast made him a little lower than the angels, and hast crowned him with glory and honour.* **(vs. 6)** *Thou madest him to have dominion over the works of thy hands: thou hast put all things under his feet:"*

Imagine the Lord of Lords and the creator of everything seated on His throne in Heaven. He had all the heavenly angels, beast, created beings and elders bowing and worship-ping before His throne, yet in the confines of His mind, He is thinking about us! He is thinking about our salvation, our lives of abundant life (Zoë life), and a life of complete victory. He is on His righteous throne crowned with glory and great wealth but is troubled when we disobey Him. He is grieved when we disappoint Him. He is touched by the very feelings of our infirmities and sickness. He even knows the very amount of hair strands on our heads. He sees them when they fall. He feeds the sparrows; we must know that He values us exceedingly more than birds who do not reflect his full image like humans do.

He loves humanity so much that while we were yet sinners He made provisions for the remission of our sins by sending Jesus to die on a cross. He gently formed us and designed our bodies in our mother's womb's and then by His Spirit drew us to know Him in salvation and by the stripes He bore through Jesus. We can be healed Hallelujah, our Father loves us eternally with an infinite unchanging love!

23

Even in His correction, He loves us. **Hebrews 12:5** *"And ye have forgotten the exhortation which speaketh unto you as unto children, My son, despise not thou the chastening of the Lord, nor faint when thou art rebuked of Him:*

> **(vs. 6)** *For whom the Lord loveth, He chasteneth, and scourgeth every son whom He receiveth.*

> **(vs. 7)** *If ye endure chastening, God dealeth with you as with sons; for what son is he whom the father chasteneth not?*

> **(vs. 8)** *But if ye be without chastisement, whereof all are partakers, then are ye bastards, and not sons."*

The writer of Hebrews declares that we should not despise the correction of our Father. As part of being a loving Father, He has to correct us if we are disobeying Him. He is also just and fair and therefore has to use measures, circumstances and sometimes situations to capture our attention to obeying Him. I am not suggesting that every bad or devastating event in our lives is an act of God's correction. Sometimes these painful experiences are the corresponding result of our own irresponsible, careless ways of living.

For example, a car accident due to drunk driving is not the act of God's correction but of violation of natural and spiritual laws.

The conviction of sin and the awareness of our mistakes by a sorrowful heart is indications of the correction that our Father uses through the Holy Spirit. He can correct us by speaking and revealing Himself in many ways. He corrects us because He does not want us to go the wrong path, eventually destroying and aborting the purposes of Christ in our lives.

He would prefer to correct us than to allow us to lose our souls and eternal salvation. In fact the writer parallels that our natural earthly fathers correct their children from a temporary understanding of the potential in them. Therefore, how much more would our heavenly father correct His children from a panoramic view because He is the only one that knows our full potential and purpose for existence. He wants to assist His Sons in fulfilling every given purpose.

The writer of Hebrews continues in that if our Heavenly Father does not convict or chasten a person; they are an outside child or a bastard. A bastard child does not have an established identity nature or inheritance. He does not carry the blessings and covering of a father, hence a father has no obligation to cultivate and increase the life of a bastard. A bastard is left to grow recklessly and lawlessly until their life is cut off and remembered no more. Aren't you glad you

Father spanks you in the Spirit every time you disobey him and calls us to repentance. Praise God!

<u>God is Love</u>

I John 4:8 *"He that loveth not knoweth not God: For God is love."*

I John 4:16 *"And we have known and believed the love that God hath to us. God is love; and he that dwelleth in love dwelleth in God and God in him."*

These verses are very interesting to understanding the nature of our Father. This writer John coined the description of our Father. He states that God is love. What an amazing global view. God does express love in His actions towards his children and creation daily. He not only thinks love, speaks love, acts in love, but His essence is love.

The *Lexical Aids* to the New Testament denotes the Greek term 'Agapáõ' (25) and Agape (26) in love:

∀ Benevolent love.

∀ It states, however, is not shown by doing what the person loved desires but what the one who loves deems as needed by the one loved;

∀ It is God's willful direction toward man.

∀ Unselfish love.

Hence, there should be a vivid mindset that every act of God is derived from His nature to love mankind. His intention toward mankind is love even in His act of discipline; God expresses His love. Even in allowing the acts of difficult circumstances, the Father has an agenda to mature His people.

John 3:16 *"For God so loved the world that He gave His only begotten Son, that whosoever believeth in Him should not perish but have everlasting life."*

The Father loved the world so dearly He gave His own Son. He has loved us eternally and intensely. We can be consumed by His everlasting Love and blessings towards us. Every aspect of our lives and its concerns can be dissolved in his oasis of love. Hallelujah!!!!

Chapter 3 End of Chapter Principles

- The Lord Jehovah is a Spirit.

- Jehovah lives in heaven as a Spiritual being but continues to be felt and experienced by mortal physical humans.

- Jehovah, Jesus and the Holy Spirit are one being.

- Jesus, as a loving father, knows our every need. He wants us to walk in the assurance that He loves us.

- The Father has His mind constantly on His precious creation man. He wants fellowship with man.

- The Father wants man to be in co-inheritance to establish Jesus' Kingdom in the earth.

- The Kingdom of God is the sovereign government and influence of Jesus in the sphere of man's existence.

Chapter 4

God as Father

!"

II Corinthians 6:16 "And what agreement hath the temple of God with idols? For ye are the temple of the living God; as God hath said, I will dwell in them, and walk in them and I will be their God, and they shall be my people."

(vs. 17) "Wherefore come out from among them, and be ye separate, saith the Lord, and touch not the unclean thing; and I will receive you,

(vs. 18) And will be a Father unto you, and ye shall be my sons and daughters saith the Lord Almighty."

God as Spiritual

Romans 1:20 *"For since the creation of the world God's invisible qualities – His eternal power and divine nature have been clearly seen, being understood from what has been made, so that men are without excuse."*

Colossians 1:15 *"Who is the image of the invisible*

God, the firstborn of every creature:

(vs. 16) *"For by Him were all things created, that are in heaven, and that are in earth, visible and invisible, whether they be thrones, or dominions, or principalities, or powers: all things were created by Him, and for Him:*

(vs. 17) *"And He is before all things, and by Him all things consist."*

I Timothy 1:17 *"Now to the King eternal, immortal, invisible the only God be honour and glory forever and ever. AMEN"*

John 4:24 *"God is spirit and His worshippers must worship in spirit and in truth."*

*O*ur Father in essence is a spiritual being; He is invisible to the eyes of humans but is very real. From a scientific point of view, I have tried to describe briefly this fact of sometime being invisible but still tangible. Our God is able to be touched and experienced by humans.

Consider the infinite amounts of creatures that surround you and live on objects around you for example there are about a million viruses that can live on the surface of the period at the end of this sentence. There are trillions of bacteria on the skin of healthy individuals can you see them? Not without the aid of a highly powered electron microscope. Consider other elements and forces around you, wind; can it be seen other than when it rushes through the leaves of trees or sweeps across your face. It cannot be seen captured in a container, but yet it is very real. Or what about electricity, you have never seen it, but yet it exists, and is very tangible. The elements and forces continue on, for example, magnetic forces are all real but have never physically been seen.

This particular nature is very vital to an understanding of our Father; how He operates and functions I am sure you are tired of the examples I gave and are probably saying, yeah what is the point? The matter is in **Genesis 1:26** *"And God said, let us make man in our image, and after our likeness: and let them have dominion over the fish, of the sea, and over the fowl of the air and over the cattle*

31

and over all the earth, and ever every creeping thing that creepeth upon the earth.

(vs. 27) *"So God created man in His own image, in the image of God created he Him: male and female created He them."*

The above scripture captures brilliantly the essences of our <u>Father</u> who is Lord, sovereign ruler and king. It describes our papa as being great and full of power.

Webster's II New Riverside Dictionary describes great as superior, outstanding, eminent or renowned. Our owner and father have a tremendous reputation of being bigger and far superior than the average false being or imaginary gods. He is known for doing grandiose acts; miracles of extreme portions and granting to His children gifts that are far above the thoughts of any human. His future plans for all creation are far beyond what our eyes have seen, ears heard or thoughts that have entered the minds of human. He is that awesome and great!

He has power

The word 'Power' comes from the *Lexical Aids* to the Old Testament numbered (2426) and (2428).

Here are the following definitions:

1. (2426) **Cheryl or Cheryl**: It means strength, valor, military force, army, wealth, virtue and honesty.

2. (2428) **Chayil** – Might, power, ability.

The main meanings of this noun are "strength", 'army' and 'wealth'.

These Old Testament commutations express a God who has strength, a military fortitude and power from wealth or influence.

New Testaments portrays the power of our Father in **Matthew 6:13** *"And lead us not into temptation but deliver us from evil: For thine is the Kingdom, and the power, and the glory, forever. AMEN."*

Revelation 4:11 *"Thou art worthy, O Lord, to receive glory and honour and power: for thou hast created all things and thy pleasure they are and were created."*

The *Lexical Aids* to the New Testament describes this power of God as:

✂ **D!namis** (1411) power. Meaning being able, capable inherent power. This means that He has built into His nature the ability and capacity to do anything. This source of enablement resides and flows from our father.

✂ **Exousia (1849) from exesti**

Romans 13:1 *"Let every soul is subject unto the higher power, for there is no power but of God: the powers that be are ordained of God."*

Jude 1:25 *"To the only wise God, our Saviour, be glory and majesty, dominion and power, both now and ever Amen."*

The word '**Exousia**' has the meaning of permission, authority, right, liberty, power to do anything. '**Exesti**' (1832) expresses the capability or the right to do a certain action.

'**Exousia**' denotes executive power or justified, having the right to exercise power. There the Greek clearly delineates that God has with Himself the power to do anything He wants. He has executive power meaning that it is His inherent right to the world and everything in it. It was not given to Him or delegated to Him power. He has power that is absolute and unrestricted.

The word dominion is another term used for our Father. It comes from the original Greek **Kr"tos** (2904), force, strength, might, more especially manifested power, dominion. '**Kr"tos**' denotes the presence and significance of force or strength.

I Chronicles 29:11 *"Yours, O Lord is the greatness and the power, and the glory and the majesty and the splendor, for everything in heaven and earth is yours. Yours, O Lord, is the Kingdom; you are exalted as head over all."*

(vs. 12) *"Wealth and honor come from you; you are the ruler of all things. In your hands are strength and power to exalt and give strength to all."*

Psalm 45:6 *"Your throne, O God, will last forever and ever; a scepter of justice will be the scripture of your Kingdom."*

Psalm 103:19 *"the Lord has established His throne in heaven and His kingdom rules over all."*

Psalm 145:13 *"Your Kingdom is an everlasting kingdom, and your dominion endures through all generations."*

Scripture clearly states that our Father is a King. A king is one who has rulership, governs and administrates sovereignty over a territory. Our Father the King from references mentioned above has sovereign rule over the earth, the creatures and over every person. All belong to the owner and master our daddy.

Our father has authority over the earth because He created the earth, the heavens and everything with those regions. He has all rights and privileges to exert His desires and will over the entire creation.

He desires to influence the world and creation with His love, righteousness, justice and holy nature thereby allowing His character to be reflected in all His creation.

A King of Wisdom

Revelation 7:11-12 *"And all the angels stood round the throne, and about the elders and the four beasts and fell before the throne on their faces, and worshipped God,* **(vs. 12)** *"Saying Amen: Blessings, and glory, and wisdom, and thanksgiving and honour and power and might be unto our God forever and ever AMEN."*

The writer John, the revelator, ascribes a glorious worth to our God. He vividly outlines a scene in the heavens that is both futuristic but yet a daily occurrence at the throne room of the Father. John articulates that angles and elders are bowing before the Lord and worshipping Him; they are giving Him the credit and worth due to His name and nature.

They are ascribing to the Father blessings (to innate ability to prosper) glory (weight of wealth and majesty) and wisdom. Our Father rules with wisdom, from His throne over the affairs of creation. He governs with great skill, understanding and wit. This word wisdom comes from the term (wisdom) (4678) – meaning true spiritual and heavenly wisdom. It also denotes skillful expert, sensible, prudent. He is a God that is very skillful in His decisions, Excellent in His operations!!

Proverbs 3:19 (NIV) *"By wisdom the Lord laid the earth's foundations, by understanding he set the heavens in place;*

(vs. 20) *"By His knowledge the deeps were divided, and the clouds let drop the dew."*

Job 12:13 *"To God belong wisdom and power; counsel and understanding are His."* We as His children can be assured and rest in the confidence that our Father rules our universe with superior ability and expertise. All decisions that are related to our faith in His direction are made in wisdom.

All things in our lives, once we abide by His laws and rules, are being carefully orchestrated by our loving father. One writer says that all things work together for our good to those persons that love the Father and are called to fulfill the purposes and will of the Father.

Even the most difficult circumstances and situations are being divinely designed to strengthen, empower, increase and propel us into God's divine destiny.

He is mindfully, strategically connecting the dots of our lives to construct a masterful piece of art work. Just trust His word!! The principles in His word, of the Bible are filled with wisdom above the knowledge of this age.

His principles and wisdom where applied consistently and continually daily will lead to a life of fulfillment and purpose. His wisdom gives us as children a tremendous advantage over the outside relatives. These 'outsiders' refers to our brothers and sisters (person who have not accepted the love of their Father through Jesus Christ as Lord and Saviour). These "bastard" children live outside of the wisdom of the Fathers plan and hence experience unnecessary pains and sufferings from the challenges of this life.

But praise God, our loving Father, we are being led by a mighty wise King who will cause His children to triumph and excel in the Kingdom He has given to us on this earth. He has given to us authority in the earth to master and challenge our lives with His eternal wisdom.

Chapter 4 End of Chapter Principles

∀ Jehovah God is an infinite spiritual being.

∀ Mankind was made in the image and likeness of the Heavenly Father as a spiritual and moral being.

∀ Jehovah has innate absolute sovereign power to rule the heaven and earth.

∀ Jehovah has executive power to govern everything.

∀ Jehovah has dominion over the earth and all the creatures (including humanity).

∀ Our Father has all wisdom; His knowledge is infinite.

Chapter 5

Daddy as King

!"

Psalm 5:2 "Hearken unto the voice of my cry, my King, and my God: for unto thee will I pray."

Psalm 10:16 "The Lord is King forever and ever: the heathen are perished out of His land."

Psalm 24:7 "Lift up your heads, O you gates; and be lifted up, ye everlasting doors, and the King of glory shall come in.

(vs. 8) "Who is this King of glory? The Lord strong and mighty, the Lord mighty in battle.

(vs. 9) Lift up your heads, O you gates; lift them up, you ancient doors that the King of glory may come in.

(vs. 10) "Who is this King of glory? The Lord of host, He is the King of glory. Selah"

*T*he word 'King' is defined by the Hebrew language as **'Malak'** (4428) **'Melek'**

A prime root meaning:

∀ To reign.

∀ To induct into royalty.

∀ To make to reign, rule, surely.

∀ King, royal.

Lexical Aids to the Old Testament denotes:

(4427) Malakh

1.) To be king, become king, rule, and reign, to consult.

2.) The essential meaning of malakl is exercising the functions of a monarch, whether as a male or a female.

'Melekh' means essentially a ruler. It can range from an emperor of an empire to the chieftain of a tiny city state.

The songwriter David begins to express the function of our Father, not only is He spirit. He is the source of our existence as the human race but the essence of our Father is a king. David begins to talk about the kingly nature. The definition point to our

Father as a ruler, a sovereign ruler, one exercising government order, administrate over a territory. This is very exciting. In scanning all major religions none of the deities have the description of being a king over creation and the universe. Our Father is great and is royalty. He has sovereignty over the earth and all those living. The passage of scripture interestingly expresses the Father as the King of glory.

What is this glory?
And how is our Father ruler of Glory?

The term '**Glory' (3513**) – kãvad or kãved; to be heavy, weighty to benumerous; to be honoured, to be renowned, to be esteemed, to show one great or mighty, to be wealthy, rich.

The key concept here is our Father who is King, is great and highly esteemed and honoured. He is wealthy with beauty, possession (goods, property, and money). What a wonderful daddy we have. He carries a lot of weight in great wealth and majesty. Consider the scriptures that articulate the tremendous ownership and possession of this king.

> **Psalm 24:1** *"The earth is the Lord's and the fullness thereof; the world and they that dwell therein.* **(vs. 2)** *"For He hath founded it on the seas, and established it upon the floods."*

I Corinthians 10:26 *"For the earth is the Lord's and the fullness thereof"*

Psalm 47: 6-9 *"Sing praises to God, sing praises; sing praises to our king, sing"***(vs. 7)** *"For God is the King of all the earth; sing ye praises with understanding."***(vs. 8)** *"God reigneth over the heathen: God sitteth upon the throne on His holiness."***(vs. 9)** *"The princes of the people are gathered together, even the people of the God of Abraham: for the shields of the earth belong unto God: He is greatly exalted."*

Psalm 95:3 *"For the Lord is the great God, the great King above all the gods."*

(vs. 4) *"In His hand are the depths of the earth, and the mountain peaks belong to Him."*

(vs. 5) *"The sea is His, for He made it, and His hands formed the dry land."*

Imagine our Father, who is endowed by nature and not delegated power, possession, wealth, and prosperity. He is a great king that is above all other kings in the earth. In fact, one writer calls Him the 'King of kings' and Lord of lords. He is described as the King that possesses nations or territories for His rulership but all the nations belong to Him.

The seas and everything in it belongs to Him. The mountains, the valleys, the streams belong to him. How about the entire world belongs to our big daddy! Wow! This should settle our hearts to every fear, anxiety, and issue of lack and poverty. All of the false gods are under his kingship. Our Father has the description of 'Lord'.

Vines Concordance definition of **'Lord'** is '**adon**' or '**adonay**' meaning '**Lord; master; Lord**." It signifies possessor or owner, one who occupies a position of authority.

Do we ever have to lack with this revelation of the Lord's kingship? If our Father is king then we are royalty; we have the genetics of majesty!! We have the DNA of kingship and splendor.

Our Father is the master and owner ('**adonay**') over the entire universe. This means we are the heirs and copartners of this earth, seas and heavens and everything in it. The scripture denotes that even the people in the earth past, present, and futuristically belongs to our father. This means that there is nothing that is in the earth that He cannot give you – Praise God!! There is no precious stone that He cannot reveal to you, no land too big that he cannot transfer to you. No person that He cannot by His command move out of your destiny. There is no person that can block the resources of what the king can give to you! We are all His possession and if we submit to the king and stay in right relationship with Him, there will be nothing impossible for us. We will be in the right partnership with the Father for a great transfer of resources. We will delve into depth later in the chapters. It is truly getting exciting as we see the revelation of the Lord unfold.

Contrary, if we are the king's own then all that we are and possess or will ever own belongs to Him. Our job, successes and accomplishments, our children, bank accounts, furniture, clothing and even our godly desires are loaned to us for stewardship of His possession. Consider at any moment He can request any possession we manage to be given over to whom He wishes for His purposes. Are we faithful enough to release everything?

Hebrews 12:5 *"And you have forgotten that word of encouragement that addresses you as sons: My son, do not make light of the Lord's discipline. And do not lose heart when he rebukes you,* **(vs. 6)** *because the Lord disciplines those He loves, and He punishes everyone He accepts as a son."*

(vs. 7) *"Endure hardship as discipline; God is treating you as sons. For what son is not disciplined by his father?* **(vs. 8)** *If you are not disciplined (and everyone undergoes discipline) then you are illegiti-mate children* and not true sons." **(vs. 9)** *"Moreover, we have all had human fathers who disciplined us and we respected them for it. How much more should we submit to the Father of our spirits and live!* **(vs.**

10) *"Our fathers disciplined us for a little while as they thought best; but God disciplines us for our good that we may share in His holiness. No discipline seems pleasant at the time, but painful. Later on, however, it produces a harvest of righteousness and peace for those who have been trained by it."*

The New Testament account of the word 'Father' from (*Lexical Aids* to the New Testament) (3962) Pater; Father.

– A spiritual Father, that is one who converts another to the Christian faith.

1.) It also means one who resembles another in disposition and actions, as children usually do their parents; an author or initiator of anything.

2.) It is spoken of God, essentially denoting the divine essence, or Jehovah, as the Creator of light of heaven.

3) As the Father of man by creation. **(Luke 3:8).**

4) He is thus called the Father of Spirits or souls.
Hebrews 12:9

James 1:17 *"Every good and perfect gift is from above, coming down from the Father of the heavenly lights, who does not change like shifting shadows.*

(vs. 18) *"He chose to give us birth through the word of truth that we might be a kind of first fruits of all He created."*

Chapter 5 End of Chapter Principles:

∀ Our heavenly Father is a King; He is a sovereign ruler and monarch.

∀ Our Father is Royalty, Majestic and has supreme rulership.

∀ God, our Father is King of Glory signifies wealth, riches, honour, and weight of possession.

∀ Our Father is King and Lord over the universe (and all creatures within.)

∀ The earth, the fullness of the earth and its inhabitants belong to our Father.

Chapter 6

A Righteous & Just Father The Father's desire and His Pleasure

!"

*P*raise the Lord we have looked at the nature, qualities and character of our Father briefly in the first few chapters. Our Father is absolutely wonderful, mighty, holy, pure, righteous, just and loving to name a few traits. He is so much more than words can even describe. He is established on a throne of majesty and dominion; He is the image of God seen in the life of Jesus Christ and yet He is also the sweet, gentle, passionate Holy Spirit. Our Father is a mighty ruler who has dominion and kingdom over the visible and invisible world; yet He has His children constantly on His mind. He made all provisions through the shed blood of Christ to save and restore man to relationship with the Father. He made us co-heirs and co-rulers over the affairs of the Father's Kingdom in the earth.

Let us now explore the desires and pleasures of our Father. Yes, He is king and a judge but He is also very passionate about fulfilling some of His most intimate dreams and visions also. Consider that concept and imagine what an amazing delight that would be for us as humans to assist in the mighty king's desires.

Wow! Firstly, let's explore some of His pleasures.

He Desires Worship

In a brief encounter with a Samaritan woman, at a well in a city called Samaria, Jesus outlines the new order for the reverence and the giving of credit to the Father. Jesus asked a woman of another race, as Jew, to give Him water. It was not a custom foe interaction with this woman a Samaritan and a Jew.

However, Jesus being the express image and fullness of the nature of our heavenly father intentionally crosses the humanity erect walls of separation and lovingly touches the disheartened soul of an emotional detach woman. This woman was in search of an identity and a heritage.

Jesus gently orchestrates the woman into relationship to her source, her Father through teaching her about what the Father really longs for. He longs for a pure heart giving worship from His children! He loves praises of sincerity, thanksgiving and honour that are wrapped in reverence into who He is.

John 4:21 *"Jesus saith unto her, Woman believe me, the hour cometh, when ye shall neither in this moun-tain, not yet at Jerusalem, worship the Father," Jesus is removing the geographical form of worship only and establishing a worship that can occur anywhere, at any time."*

(vs. 22) *"Ye worship ye know not what: we know what we worship: for salvation is of the Jews."*

(vs. 23)*"But the hour cometh and now is when the true worshippers shall worship the Father in spirit and in truth: for the Father seeketh such to worship him."*

Amazing, the Father seeks for persons to worship Him in Spirit and in truth.

The scriptures record that the eyes of the Lord seeketh to and fro for worshippers in the earth. It also outlines that He dwells in the praises of His people. He come down and becomes enthroned in our midst.

Psalm 22:3 *"But thou art holy, O thou, that inhabits the praises of Israel."*

Psalm 145:1 *"I will extol thee, my God, O king; and I will bless thy name forever and ever."*

(vs. 2)*"Every day will I bless thee; and I will praise thy name forever and ever."***(vs. 3)** *"Great is the Lord, and greatly to be praised; and His great-ness is unsearchable."* **(vs. 4)** *"One generation shall praise thy works to another, and shall declare thy mighty acts."* **(vs. 5)** *"I will speak of the glorious honour of thy majesty, and of thy wondrous works."*

(vs. 6) *"And men shall speak of the might of thy terrible acts: and I will declare thy greatness."*

(vs. 10) *"All thy works shall praise thee, O Lord; and thy saints shall bless thee."*

(vs. 11) *"They shall speak of the glory of thy kingdom, and talk of thy power;*

(vs. 12) *"To make known to the sons of men his mighty acts, and the glorious majesty of His Kingdom."* **(vs. 13)** *"Thy kingdom is an everlasting kingdom, and thy dominion endureth throughout all generations."*

Daddy's Delight

Psalm 35:27 *"Let them shout for joy, and be glad that favor my righteous cause: yea, let them say continually, Let the Lord be magnified, which hath pleasure in the prosperity of his servant."*

Our daddy has a few secrets about Him that as a Son, I will reveal to the other family members. He has pleasures, He enjoys certain things and we are going to explore those areas. The King loves to be pleasured by His creation.

Earlier, we saw that daddy loves worship and praise not only from His creation but from humans. He sings over us and we sing unto Him. Our Father does not need to be any bigger than He is, but He loves when we honour and adore Him by our own free will. He loves when we acknowledge as humans that He is the source of our very existence! He is jealous over our worship and adoration. He knows that our worship establishes the knowledge that we did not create ourselves and that we must fully trust Him. As a king who has lordship over His subjects who are also His children; our worship obliges the Father to provide, protect and sustain us Hallelujah!!

He also has pleasures to be received. The word plea-sure from the Hebrew gives a clear picture of His emotional nature. The *Lexical Aids* to the Old Testament **'Chaphets'** (2654) means to:

1) "To take delight in.

2) Be pleased with.

3) Have affection for...

4) To desire, like...

5.) To feel a strong positive attraction for something."

Our Father has strong desires and affections. The next few words truly impressed me. Usually, a person would have a desire for a particular food such as ice-cream, a favou-rite television show or movie. For example even a particular fragrance or colour. However, our God desires to see His children prosper. Wow!

Our Father sits on His throne and longs for a sincere passion to see His children increase in every area of their lives. He is constantly talking, instructing, directing and ordering the necessary plans needed them. He gets enjoyment when His sons inherit every promise and goodness in their lives and the life to come.

James 1:17 *"Every good gift and every perfect gift is from above, and cometh down from the Father of lights with whom is no variableness, neither shadow of turning."*

This scripture brilliantly expounds that all good things are those made available by the hand of the Father. The gift of life, health, liberty, strength to achieve goals, the right connections of persons to propel us into our destiny, He strategically sets in order. In fact, our Father allows the rain or the goodness of life to be made available to the just and unjust person. He so loves that He allows His good nature and resources to be given to those who do love Him and refuse to honour Him. What a loving Father!

The word prosperity (7965) comes from the Hebrew 'Shalom' (*Lexical Aids* to the Old Testament). **1)** 'Shalom' means health, security, tranquility, welfare and good condi-tion. This word carries the embodiment success, comfort, peace, whole, secure, safe, happy and sound. **2)** A state of well-being. The *reference dictionary* depicts shalom "as a satisfied condition, an unconcerned state of peacefulness. **'Shalom'** is a harmonious state of soul and mind both externally and internally. The writer states in the *Lexical Aids* that to wish one shalom implies a blessing.

The root word of Shalom is Shalam (7999) meaning to be whole, to be sound, be safe, to keep safe, to make secure, and to live in harmony with God. God our father sits in the heaven lies and has a sincere passion to see the health of His children. The Scripture records a number of interesting outlines that expresses this concern the Father has for the physical well-being of His people. Health describe by most dictionaries or reference books 'is the state of well-being, physically, mentally, emotionally, and spiritually and not just the absence of disease.'

He says I am the Lord that healeth your diseases and another place the scripture records in **Isaiah 53:5** *"But He was wounded for our transgressions He was bruised for our iniquities: the chastisement of our peace was upon Him; and with His stripes we are healed."*

Our Father does not only want His people to receive divine supernatural healing but walk in a continuous flow of the anointing of health. The Father has made provision already by the shed blood of Jesus Christ. We have the right and the Father's sincere passion to walk whole.

Therefore, reject every illness and disease that tries to manifest in the body of your family or your life. Stand on the "Shalom" word spoken over your life. Stand up in the father's desire for your life and allow His word to line up with your body and mind. This health also encompasses the mental well-being of His children. Daddy delights when His children can rest and sleep stress-free. He wants comfort in the time of trouble.

> **Isaiah 26:3-4** *"Thou wilt keep him in perfect peace, whose mind is stayed on thee: because he trusteth in thee.*
>
> **(vs. 4)** *"Trust ye in the Lord forever: for in the Lord JEHOVAH is everlasting strength."*

He will maintain our complete soundness and peace if we remember His heart's desire and plan for us to continually be whole in our mind. Jesus expresses emphatically in Matthew's account of the Gospel Jesus' desire, the Father's heart that His Sons walk in the mental peace and wholeness amidst any challenging or distressing situations.

> **Matthew 11:28** *"Come unto me, all ye that labour and are heavy laden, and I will give you rest."* **(vs. 29***) "Take my yoke upon you, and learn of me; for I am meek, and lowly in heart: and ye shall find rest unto your souls."*

There is a place of rest or settling when we turn to Jesus Christ. And again the word records, **Psalm 127:2** *"It is vain for you to rise up early, to sit up late, to eat the bread of sorrows: for so He giveth His beloved sleep."*

Well let us examine our Father's thought's concerning His Sons under the desires of the Papa. **Psalm 139:17** *"How precious also are thy thoughts unto me, O God! How great is the sum of them!"*

(vs. 18) *"If I should count them, they are more in numbers than the sands: when I awake, I am still with thee."*

His mind is filled with the wonders of how He is going to bless us. They are so numerous they would compare with the amount of sand on seashore. He thinks about the complete wholeness of His children. Praise God!!!

Chapter 6 End of Chapter Principles

∀ Our Father is holy pure, righteous and is a just King.

∀ Our Heavenly Father desires the act of worship. Worship is the act of giving value to something of significant worth.

∀ A King as our Father desires honour, praise, thanks and worship from His subjects.

∀ Worship is and act fitting to one whom has power over your life and all creation. Our father is a King deserving of honour.

∀ Our Father delights in the prosperity of His people. He wants His sons to be successful.

∀ Our Father desire's the 'Shalom' complete wholeness of life to be the model of His children's lives.

Chapter 7

Papa's Prosperity Plan

!"

Deuteronomy 8:18 "But thou shalt remember the Lord thy God: for it is He that giveth thee power to get wealth, that He may establish His covenant which He swore unto thy fathers, as it is on this day."

The Scripture declares that we ought to always remember our owner and source. It is through His ability, enablement, access and authority that we get the wealth. He gives His ability, His word, principles and strength for His children to acquire not only physical, emotional, and mental well-being but also financial wealth, praise God!

Father comes to live with His children

John 14:16-20 *"And I will pray the Father, and he shall give you another Comforter, that he may abide with you forever. Even the Spirit of truth; whom the world cannot receive, because it seeth him not, neither knoweth him: but ye know him; for he dwelleth with you and shall be in you."*

(vs. 18) *"I will not leave comfortless: I will come to you."*

(vs. 19) *"Yet a little while, and the world seeth me no more, but ye see me: because I live, ye shall live also."*

(vs. 20) *"And that day ye shall know that I am in my Father, and ye in me, and I in you."*

John 14:26-27 *"But the Comforter, which is the Holy Ghost, whom the Father will send in my name, he shall teach you all things, and bring all things to your remembrance, whatsoever I have said unto you."*

(vs. 27) *"Peace I leave with you, my peace I give unto you: not as the world giveth, give I unto you..."*

John 15:26-27 *"But when the Comforter is come, whom I will send unto you from the Father, even the Spirit of truth, which proceedeth from the Father, He shall testify of me."*

(vs. 27) *"And ye also shall bear witness, because ye have been with me from the beginning."*

John 16:13-16 *"Howbeit when He, the Spirit of truth, is come, He will guide you unto all truth: for He shall not speak of Himself; but whatsoever He shall hear, that shall He speak; and He will show you things to come."*

(vs. 14) *"He shall glorify me: for He shall receive of mine, and shall shew it unto you.*

(vs. 15) *"All things that the Father hath are mine: therefore said I, that He shall take of mine, and shall shew it unto you.*

(vs. 16) *"A little while, and ye shall not see me: and again, a little while, and ye shall see me, because I go to the Father.*

Daddy is filled with gifts and wonderful surprises for His Sons. He has provided all things for them to enjoy and share. The Father mysteriously now presents the greatest gift of all to His precious children.

I can imagine a wonderful birthday of a young boy as he wakes early and runs excitedly to his parent's bedroom. He is eagerly anticipating the promise of his father. All year long the young lad cleaned his room on time, washed the dishes and did his homework in excellence. Now it was his time to be the recipient of reward by his father. He gently knocks on the bedroom door of his Father and shouts, "Dad, Dad!" his father having anticipated the son's desire for the promised gift cries, "Come on in son!" His son raced through the doors as a horse out of a Kentucky Derby starting gate and galloped towards his father. He leaped into the bed in between his mother and father and melodiously sang, "Did you remember dad?" in the ears of the Father. Lovingly the father stared at his handsome 10-year-old son whose eyes now beamed with joy and whose smile was wider than the Nile River; he replied yes. The father said happy birthday and gently embraced the boy. The Father hurried into a nearby bedroom closet and rolled into the room a 10 speed mountain bicycle sparkling blue with gold trimmings to the lad. His eyes lit up with magnificence as his father said joyously this is your gift son; I remembered my promised. Without hesitation the son jumped on the bicycle; his father stood by with a smile as was overwhelm with the excitement of the son. Immediately the writer Luke's analogy popped into my mind; and clearly outlined the nature of the Father.

> **Luke 11:13** *"If you then, being evil, know how to give good gifts unto your children: how much more shall your heavenly Father give the Holy Spirit to them that ask Him?"*

Jesus strongly states that men and earthly fathers are moved with fulfillment when they give their children gifts. They get joy from things that would make them happy, increase their value and gifts that would propel their children dreams. Jesus reveals the agape level of love in this verse; in that the heavenly Father gives the most powerful person and tool for the ultimate fulfillment of purpose of His children.

The Heavenly Father gives Himself in the person of the Holy Spirit to dwell with His Sons forever. Let us clarify how He does this mysterious and marvelous event.

The writer John in **I John 5:7**, *"For there are three that bear record in heaven, the <u>Father</u>, the <u>Word</u> and the <u>Holy Ghost</u>: and these three are one."*

(vs. 11) *"And this is the record that God hath given to us eternal life, and this life is in His son."*

(vs. 12) *"He that hath the Son hath life: and he that hath not the Son of God hath not life."*

John expresses that the Father, the Word (Jesus) and the Holy Spirit are one. They have the same vision but different functions but yet still remain the same. It is a mystery!!! There is then eternal life in the Son as the Son gives us the Holy Spirit as we will examine. The Father knows how to give the gift of Himself to be an advisor forever with His Sons in the Earth. John the writer records the most profound words of Jesus as He expresses the wondrous plans and purposes of the Father towards mankind.

In **John 14:15-20 (vs. 15)** *"If ye love me, keep my commandments,*

(vs. 16) *"And I will pray the Father and He shall give you another Comforter that he may abide with you forever;***(vs. 17)** *"Even the Spirit of truth; whom the world cannot receive, because it seeth Him not, neither knoweth Him, but ye know Him; for He dwelleth with you, and shall be in you."***(vs. 18)** *"I will not leave you comfortless: I will come to you."*

(vs. 19) *"Yet a little while, and the world seeth me no more; but ye see me: because I live ye shall live also."***(vs. 20)** *"At that day ye shall know that I am in my Father, and ye in me, and I in you."*

(vs. 21) *"He that hath my commandments, and keepeth them, he it is that loveth me: and he that loveth me shall be loved of my Father and I will love him, and will manifest myself to him."*

Here is the passion and intent of the Father that by abiding and living by the commandments the Father will give His Sons the Holy Spirit. Here we see Jesus petitioning the Father to send the perfect gift of the Holy Spirit to be with the believer forever. Praise God! Jesus truly gives His best to His Sons. The Holy Spirit—man's greatest gift!!

Amazingly, Jesus elaborated on the relationship of the Holy Spirit with His children; the Holy Spirit will not just rest upon the believer temporally or visit the children of God in a Sunday service. Neither will He just show up to give the believer a jump or a shout. The Holy Spirit was given to the Sons of God to dwell in the children hearts. He will be their closest confidant, friend and advisor.

What an awesome privilege!! Sadly, the world, the bastard children, those not in conventional relation or identity with the Father cannot see Him, the Holy Spirit or perceive Him. The Father was so concerned and mindful of His intimate relationship, He did not want to leave us anymore. He wanted to be next to and inside His children forever. Praise God He has far surpassed any earthly father or false God. There is no other claim of other gods as Jesus' claims of what the Father has done by living in His children forever.

> **John 14:19** expresses the uninterrupted relation-ship the Father wants. He states that He would never leave His children comfortless; meaning there will never be a moment that He wants His Sons to be out of peace with themselves or external circumstances. Jesus begins to speak about the gift of the Holy Spirit and the intermixing He wants for Sons with the Father and the Holy Spirit. **Verse 20** states, *"At that day ye shall know that I am in my Father, and ye in me and I in you."*

Praise God, the Father with Jesus and the gift (Holy Spirit) desire oneness that would cause a power unity a marriage that would complete the love relationship of the Father.

In fact, Jesus promises that the sons that keep the commandments and love Him will have reciprocal love streaming down from His throne that will saturate their lives. Jesus will also flood His sons with an abundance of 'agape' love relationship love and concern. He will also reveal His nature, purpose and secrets to the obedient Sons.

> **John 14:26** *"But the Comforter, which is the Holy Ghost, whom the Father will send in my name, He shall teach you all things, and bring all things to your remembrance, whatsoever I have said unto you."*

> **John 15:26** *"But the comforter is come, whom I will send unto you from the Father, even the Spirit of truth, which proceeded from the Father, He shall testify of me."*

John expounds that the gift, the Holy Spirit has functions while He lives and abides in the life of the believer.

Jesus describes the Holy Spirit in **John 16:14-15**, *"He shall glorify me: for He shall receive of mine, and shall show it unto you."*

> **(vs. 15)** *"All things that the Father hath are mine: therefore said I, that he shall take of mine, and shall shew it unto you.*

The key to developing any firm relationship is communication. This involves both verbal and nonverbal uses of symbols, language and speech to portray one's concept and meaning. This form of communication the Father wanted expressed by Jesus is a constant dialogue with His Holy Spirit. He knew that He was returning to the Heavenly Father after completing His purpose and mission in the earth and was about to engage in a new work as the Chief Intercessor for the Sons of God.

Our heavenly Father's intention for the creation was relationship and not a dictatorship for man. The Father sent the gift of the Holy Spirit to assist in cultivating and maintaining a line of communication and intimacy with His children. Amidst intimacy come strong family ties, identity as with a clearer understanding of the other persons involved. With the contents of a natural family, moments share in activity or simply talking forges bonds between members. These bonds are emotional and individuals have the opportunity to express feelings of anger, disappointment, satisfaction and joy in a loving environment. The Lord our Father is quite the same; desiring to be an active father, friend, confidant in our lives.

He desires to reward obedience, correct our errors and foster our dreams and destinies. There is a tremendous blessing for obedience to the voice of the Spirit of our Father.

John 17:25, *"O righteous Father, the world had not known thee: but I have known thee, and these have known that thou have sent me."* The Father's intention for His prize children He created was for intimated relationship and fellowship and not dicta-torship. Let us look at the Father's yearning to be our sources, progenitor and daily nourisher through the Holy Spirit.

II Corinthians 6:16-18 *"And what agreement hath the temple of God with idols? For ye are the temple of the living God; as God hath said, I will dwell in them, and walk with them; and I shall be their God, and they shall be my people."*

(vs. 17) *"Wherefore come out from among them, and be ye separate, saith the Lord, touch not the unclean thing; and I will receive you,*

(vs. 18) *And will be a Father unto you, and ye shall be my sons and daughters saith the Lord Almighty."*

Paul the writer of Corinthians challenges the church at Corinth to avoid being unequally yoked together with unbe-lievers in **verse fourteen**. He unlocks the mysterious of Christ and the indwelling of the Holy Spirit sent from the Father in the believer. Paul metaphorically relates our bodies as the temple or the place where the divine meets the natural man, of the Father.

"… Ye are the temple of the living God…"

The Holy Spirit who is living, a being that lives, feels, is offended desires to live in the Sons. He the Holy Spirit says *"I will dwell in them and walk in them…"* Amazing He will be their God. The Almighty King of the Universe states, that *"He shall be the faithful father unto His Sons and daughters."* He has taken full responsibility of being the source of all His children. Praise God saints, you don't have to look into the oblivion of the skies and seek daddy. Just realize that His Holy Spirit is right next to you to hear all of your concerns. He wants to celebrate with your victories and successes in life; grieve with you hurt and comfort you in distress.

Praise God look inside you; He dwells not in the temple of stones as in the old covenant, but through the request of Jesus, He lives forever in us His Sons!

Praise God look this moment and acknowledge the presence of the Holy Spirit right next to you as you read these words and worship the King and Father who abides in your inner being. Go on just love on Him for a minute.

The children of God are as carriers of royalty, majesty, glory and transporters of the King. We change the atmosphere when you step into a room or circumstance because you carry the God in you. Every circumstance of life must bow in the presence of the King. Greater is He that is in you than any person or situation facing you. You are a God carrier of His glorious presence! Sons are an ark of the presence of God.

Chapter 7 End of Chapter Principles

∀ Our heavenly father is infinitely wealthy and wants to share His riches with His children in the earth.

∀ The father's greatest gift is to His entrance in the earth as Jesus.

∀ The Father's awesome gift was to live inside the life of every believer of Jesus Christ.

∀ The Father dwells in His sons as the Holy Spirit.

∀ The Holy Spirit is the director advisor and comforter who is the exact nature as Jesus.

∀ The Holy Spirit of Jesus only speaks and directs in the purpose of the Father.

∀ Humans can now connect with the destiny of the Father for them through submission to the Holy Spirit.

Chapter 8

The Sweet Comforter

!"

*John 14:26 "But the Comforter, which is the Holy
Ghost, whom the Father will send in my name, He
shall teach you all things..."*

In the book, *Knowing the Doctrine of the Bible* (Myer Pearlman) writes that, "The Holy Spirit proceeds from God, is sent from God, and is God's gift to men. Yet the Spirit is not independent of God. He always represents the one God acting in the spheres of thought, will, and activity."

The Spirit of Jesus is sent in the name of Christ. The Spirit is the person of spiritual life by which men are born unto the Kingdom of Jesus. This new life of the Spirit is imparted and maintained by Christ's Holy Spirit living in followers of Jesus.

The *Lexical Aids* to the New Testament denotes the word **'Comforter'** as **'Parakletos'** (3875) from the root word **'Parakaléō'** (3870). **Parakaléō** comes from two words **'para'**, by the side and **'kaléō'** – to call; to call to ones side, hence aid.

1) Used for every kind of calling to a person which is intended to produce a particular effect; comfort, exhort, desire, call for, an appeal.

2) An encouragement, exhortation, consolation, and comfort.

Hence the concept is **'Parakalétōs'** (3875) meaning a legal advisor, pleader, proxy, or an advocate, one who comes forward on behalf of and as the representative of another.

Jesus Christ in His prayer for the Holy Spirit assigns Him as equal to the Father and Jesus. The Holy Spirit continues the function of the Sons of God in the earth, acting in the same manner and purpose if Jesus were still physically in the earth.

The word 'comforter' or Greek "Parakletos" bears the following literal meaning. One called to the side of another for the purpose of assisting him in any way particularly in legal and criminal hearings. It was the custom in ancient tribunals for parties to appear in court attended by one or more of their most influential close friends, who were called in Greek 'Paracletos'. These give their intimate friends – not for money or reward, but from love and concern. They gave advance of their personal presence and the aid of their wise counsel. They advised them on actions, verbal response, and spoken advice and acted on their interest. They made the plight of their friends their own cause, stood by them and on behalf of them in the trials and difficulties. Jesus left them with the promise of another comforter who should be our defender, helper, and teacher during His absence. The Holy Spirit is thus both Jesus Christ's successor but also His majestic presence. Since God is a Spirit and they that worship Him (or communicate to Him worthy) must worship Him in spirit and truth, the Holy Spirit establishes residents in the Sons.

Now the rivers of love and wisdom can stream directly from the throne of the Father into the connected channels of man's hearts through the Holy Spirit. Praise God!! The Holy Spirit acts as the generator that propels and models man into the image of Christ Jesus. The Holy Spirit also activates powers and ushers the power of attorney to the believer. The Sons cannot only communicate with the Father but can legally conduct the interest, property, business, and governmental affairs of the Kingdom of God in the earth.

The Father's nature and wisdom pre-arranged the sending of the precious person of the Holy Spirit to the children; to equip them to effectively communicate and worship Him. The Father desires to fellowship with His children; yet He still loves when they thank Him and give Him due honour for all that He is and does. Praise God!

So then the Father sends the Holy Spirit to help His Sons to access the presence of the Father. The Holy gift (the Holy Spirit) activates our Spirit to worship the Father through relationship, revelation, and true understanding of who He is and who we are in Him. **John 4:23,** *"But the hour cometh and now is when the true worshippers shall worship the Father in spirit and in truth: for the Father seeketh such to worship Him."* **(vs. 24)** *"God is a spirit: and they that worship Him must worship Him in spirit and in truth."*

Chapter 8 End of Chapter Principles

∀ The Holy Spirit is the person of Jesus Christ in the earth.

∀ The Holy Spirit is the same nature character and essence of Jesus our Father.

∀ The Holy Spirit is the legal advisor, advocate, director and teacher of the Sons of God.

∀ The Holy Spirit lives in the believer of Jesus Christ.

∀ Those who want to worship must do it with inner truth.

Chapter 9

The Father's Heart desire and purpose is To give His children His Kingdom

---

!"

The Father has an unselfish heart and deep passion to enter into an eternal partnership with His sons in the management of all His Kingdom. Daddy wants to entrust sons as trustees in the earth and marketplaces to establish righteous rule and laws in all areas of human interaction. Even more glorious is that He also wants to entrust His sons as heirs with God and co-heir in the rule and reign in the Kingdom to come. Praise God!!

One writer profoundly articulates that a wise father leaves an inheritance for His children and children's children. Our heavenly Father is the prototype of the fatherhood and does the exact same principle of giving an inheritance to His children. He gives the inheritance to His children and generations thereafter. He gives the inheritance of <u>iden-tity</u>, <u>ownership</u>, <u>rule ship</u>, <u>partnership</u> and <u>fellowship</u> to His Sons.

Let us examine those concepts briefly from the scriptures account of God's inheritance to man.

> **Genesis 1:26** *"And God said, let us make man in our image, after our likeness: and let them have dominion over the fish of the sea, and over the cattle, and over all the earth and over every creeping thing that creepeth upon the earth."*

> **(vs. 27)** *"So God <u>created</u> man in His own image, in the image of God created he him, <u>male</u> and <u>female</u> created He them."*

> **(vs. 28)** *"And God blessed them and God said unto them, be fruitful, and multiply, and replenish the earth and subdue it and have dominion over the fish of the sea, and over the fowl of the air, and over every living thing that moveth upon the earth."*

> **(vs. 29)** *"And God said, Behold, I have given you every herb bearing seed, which is upon the face of all the earth and every tree yielding seed; to you it shall be meat."*

There are astounding relations locked into these few verses in which many great generals in the body of Christ have unlocked over the ages. Many have uncovered the original intent of God for man, the ruler ship authority and position of man; the delegated stewardship of man over the earth and its resources.

For this book purpose let us examine **Genesis 1:26-30:**

1. Image of mankind.

2. Dominion of mankind.

3. Ownership of Mankind.

4. Empowered to prosper by God over humanity.

Our Father like any other earthly male usually wants to continue His seed and lineage throughout the generations. Our Father did that by forming man with His spiritual DNA. Enclose within every human being is the genetic code of their father. In science, the genetic code can be divided into the genotype and the phenotype. Scientists, we concur that the genotype is not always seen in the physical outside appearance of an offspring. This means that by simply looking at a species it is not obvious at times that it came from a particular parent. Hence, a complex study has to be taken from a species, for example, a blood sample, analyzed and genetic code determined. However, the phenotype is the external physical characteristic that portrays the features of its parent's appearance. For example a person's blood, hair along with other distinct features of its parents in humans.

This analogy represents the offspring of the heavenly Father; there are many who don't have the express image and nature of the Father through Jesus Christ. Yet there are those who not only carry the concealed DNA of the Father but also express the nature, love, character authority and dominion of Him.

John 4:24 states that *"God is a spirit..."* Hence man being in the image and likeness of God must be a spirit and merely possess a spirit. The Father then gives man dominion of Kingdom rule over the earth and its creatures.

The dominion man was given best be interpreted from *Lexical Aids* to the Old Testament 7287 **('Radah') meaning to 'tread down' (as a wine press, with the feet); to subju-gate, subdue.**

It also expresses the meaning, **to crumble, rule cause to rule, have reign over and prevail against.** Hence, the Father created man with the same nature as He is being a King and Lord, full with authority, power, and ruler ship. He then gives man the territory to reign based on the fore knowledge that the essence of governance is in man. He is aware that man's genetic code enables them to subdue life and manage the resources of earth. The Father moves into a greater love support by proclaiming and empowering man to prosper.

Genesis 1:28 *"And God blesses them, and God said unto them, "Be fruitful and multiply and replenish the earth and subdue it."*

The Father extended His favour, grace and release of goodness to flow on the life of His first created son Adam and his offspring. He commanded His sons to bring about increase harvest replication of all that is with the Godly essence in man and cause it to manifest and fill the earth. His sons were to then govern the products of man's invention, the earth and environment in accordance with the laws and nature of our righteous Father and King.

Daniel, the prophet hundreds of years after the relinquishing of man's dominion to Satan recalls the original intent of the Father in:

Daniel 7:18 *"But the saints of the Most High shall take the Kingdom, and possess the Kingdom forever, even forever and ever."*

Daniel 7:27 *"And the Kingdom and dominion, and the greatness of the Kingdom under the whole heaven, shall be* *given to the people of the saints of the Most High, whose Kingdom is an everlasting Kingdom, and all dominions shall serve and obey Him."*

Exodus 19:5 *"Now therefore, if ye will obey my voice indeed, and keep my covenant, then ye shall be a peculiar treasure unto me above all people: for all the earth is mine:"*

(vs. 6) *"And ye shall be unto me a kingdom of priests, and a holy nation. These are the words which thou shalt speak unto the children of Israel."*

The Father clearly expresses through the vision and prophecies to Daniel the sons of the Most High will possess the Kingdom. The term the prophet used is the word *"saints;"* this does not refer to a selected group of persons who an organization defined.

Contrary, according to the *Lexical Aids* to the Old Testament saint (6922) means **Qadosh (6918) and Qadash** (6942). **'Qadosh'** means sacred, selected, pure, holy, conse-crated, and pious.

Hence the concept is a group of persons set aside, conse-crated unto the purpose and calling of the Heavenly Father. The Father's Holy sons, who have separated themselves unto the work, character and obedience to the Father, will possess the Kingdom of God.

'**Q"d"sh**' (6942) express a similar meaning to be hallow, dedicated, holy, purify and consecrated to God. It signifies an act or a state in which people or things are set aside for use in the worship of God. Therefore the mature Sons who have continuous obedience and fellowship with the Father will inhabit the Kingdoms.

The Old Testament definition of the Kingdom the saints will possess is derived from the Hebrew '**malkût**' (4438), **Kingdom; reign and rule.**

The word denotes **1.)** The territory of the Kingdom. **2.)** The accession to the throne. **3.)** Anything Royal or Kingly.

Lexical Aids to the Old Testament describes **('malkhuth'**

– 4438) as a dominion, an empire a Kingdom, a realm, a reign, royal rule and sovereign power. 'Malkhuth' comes from the noun 'M!lakh' (4427) meaning to be King. The essential understanding of M!lakh is exercising the func-tions of a monarchy or royal authority. M!lakh can be the act of God or men in exalting a person to the office of royalty.

Hence the concept of the father giving His Sons a territory in which they can exercise kingly rule and sovereign power to govern other words that express the Father's desire for His children is the words from *Vines*

Complete Expository Dictionary: *Basileia* (Kingship; Kingdom; royal power). Another translation of the kingdom is the words **mamil"k"h** (4467) signifies **kingdom, sover-eignty; dominion; reign.**

The basic meaning of *'manil!k!h'* is the area and people that constitute a Kingdom. It can also be synonym nouns to nation. Manil!k!h can also denotes, "Kings" as the king was considered to be the embodiment of the "Kingdom."

The Old Testament further defines as expressions of the royal "rule" all things associated with the king:

Throne:

The throne expresses the symbolic head of the state, territory, royal rule and governance over a territory. It is a seat of power, influence and wealth and our Heavenly Father wants to give His rule over the natural and spiritual realm to His obedient Sons- Praise Jesus!

> **Luke 12:32** *"Fear not little flock; for it is your Father's good pleasure to give you the Kingdom."*

Jesus confirms to the disciples and spoke into the lives of the sons throughout the ages who sometimes become concerned about daily living.

The descriptions "Father's good pleasure" unlocks the fervent love and concern, daddy has for His children. The term according to *Lexical Aids* to the New Testament is **Eudok#$ (2106)** from **eu** well good and **dek#$** to think something good; not merely an understanding of what is right and good but stressing the willingness and freedom of an intention or resolve regarding what is good."

Here we understand that the Father extends benevolence, a gracious purpose to give His sons the royal rulership over the works He created. Hallelujah to our Father!

Chapter 9 End of Chapter Principles

∀ The Father desires to establish His dominion ruler-ship in the earth under the entire universe is under the entire universe is under His righteous influence.

∀ The Father wants His righteous influence to reign and rule in the earth.

∀ The Kingdom of God is activated in any person through acceptance of Jesus Christ as 'Lord'.

∀ The Holy Spirit is sent as the promise to the believer in Jesus Christ. The Holy Spirit connects the communication between heaven and earth.

∀ The Holy Spirit works to mature infants in the faith to adult Sons

∀ Matured Sons execute the Father's will purpose and agenda in the earth partnering with the Holy Spirit.

∀ **Sons are saints (selected, consecrated, set apart individuals.)**

∀ **It is the Father's good pleasure to give His children His Kingdom.**

Chapter 10

The Father as Holy and Perfect (He is the same yesterday, today and forever)

!"

The Father is very diverse in His nature; it is incomprehensive to think that He can even be contained in the books or writings of men. However, due to the Father's everlasting love, to establish an intimate and covenantal relationship with His children He has revealed parts of His nature throughout the confines of time. He also uses the marvelling of life circumstances to show his glory.

The songwriter writes that the heavens declare His nature and glory. Let us examine another vital character of our Father in the scriptures of the biblical text. Scripture states in **Isaiah 6:3** that the prophet saw a scene in the heavens of glorious angels declaring. *"And one cried unto another, and said Holy, Holy, Holy, is the Lord of host: the whole earth is full of His glory."*

Again an awesome picturesque view painted in Revelation chapter four of the magnificent Father. He is seated on His throne in heaven with the appearance of precious jewels of jasper and surrounded by rainbows of emerald.

Revelations 4:1-3 *"After this I looked, and, behold, a door was opened in heaven: and the first voice which I heard was as it were of a trumpet talking with me..."*

(vs. 2) *"And immediately I was in the spirit: and behold, a throne was set in heaven, and one sat on the throne."*

(vs. 3) *"And He that sat was to look upon like jasper and a sardine stone and there was a rainbow round about the throne in sight like unto an emerald."*

These next few verses vividly detail the wondrous worship and celebration of our Father the king in the heavens. The writer John of revelation brilliantly articulates the splendor of an activity around the throne of the King.

Revelation 4:8 *"And the four beasts had each of them six wings about him; and they were full of eyes within: and they rest not day and night saying Holy, holy, holy, Lord God Almighty, which was and is, and is to come."*

(vs. 9) *"And when those beasts give glory and honour and thanks to Him that sat on the throne, who liveth forever and ever,*

(vs. 10) *The four and twenty elders fall down before Him that sat on the throne, and worship Him that liveth forever and ever, and cast their crowns before the throne, saying,*

(vs. 11) *"Thou art worthy, O Lord, to receive glory and honor and power: for thou hast created all things, and for thy pleasure they are and were created."*

Majesty, what a detailed visualization of what we should be doing on the earth to match the worship of the king in heaven. If the angels and created being can fall on their bodies and lie prostrate and give glory and honour from their lips continually; certainly we the redeemed and blood-washed believer should have a greater praise for our salvation.

From the text, let us examine the term Holy as an essence of our Father's character. The term Holy (40) according to the *Lexical Aids* to the New Testaments is derived from the Greek *Hagios* meaning:

🖋 Set apart.

🖋 Sanctified.

🖋 Consecrated.

🖋 Chaste and pure.

Our Father's nature gives the idea of being pure; free from contamination and defilement. He has no evil or sin in His nature. One writer states that God does not tempt; neither can be tempted to evil. He is set apart from all forms of perversion. The concept then is our Father God is totally pure in words, deeds, mindset, action, motives and decisions. His words and actions are consistent and coherent to His professed nature. Praise the Lord our Father means what He says, acts in purity and will fill every word that He has promised His sons.

Father as Perfect

Matthew 5:48 *"Be ye therefore perfect, even as your Father which is in heaven is perfect."*

This scripture outlines two concepts 1. Perfect from the *Lexical Aids* to New Testament is **'Teleios' from 'Telos' (5056**) - has the meaning of the end, goal the fullness or finality of the process of development of a thing. To clarify this term it gives the expression of the fullness, maturity or completeness of a thing. In this case, it suggests the complete-ness and total wholesome nature of our God. One writer calls Him the ancient of Days. There is no more growing or maturing learning or increasing of our Father. He is all the fullness of what He should be now. This concept is difficult to parallel in nature and human life because we exist in a changing world. The environment is constantly changing, time is moving and rolling into the future, the seasons and cycles of weather and climates fluctuate daily. Even humans are not static but change views, opinions, ideas, even behav-iour on a daily basis. There are changes in the weight, height and needs of humans daily.

The world economies and stock markets are grossly dynamic; but only our Father, our Lord Jesus Christ and the Holy Spirit remain constant. Praise God He is the same yesterday, today and forever. His word remains the same throughout eternity. He is not a respecter of persons; He hates sin and judges rightly. It does not matter what humanity says about sin; including abortion, sexual perversion, homosexuality and corruption, our king's law and views remained the same from eternity to eternity. He will never speak or act or accept the perversion of mankind if it violates His world or nature.

He is Holy!

The word 'Teleios' (5046) describes 'perfect' as the following:

🖋 Full growth

🖋 Completed growth

🖋 God's perfection is absolute and man's nature and being is relative. He has reached His mortal end.

Jesus commands us in the above text of Matthew, to be perfect. This seems possibly overwhelming to be whole in every situation. This does not mean there will not be challenges of life or difficult times that seem to stretch our faith and walk in Christ.

Jesus declares this instruction to us because He knows that through the power of the blood of Jesus and the strength of the Holy Spirit we can overcome. The Sons of God can be matured sons and daughters as their heavenly father is, matured whole, pure and live in integrity. This is one of the ways our lives as sons can reflect the invisible Father who lives in a realms that is outside of our natural tangible touch many times. It is even more difficult for an unbelieving world that is unaware of their inheritance as sons of God in Christ to even see the King their Father and all He has stored in the Kingdom. We must all be born again through Christ to even begin to understand and grasp the perfect and loving nature of the Father who lives in the heavens.

We can be the agents; the mirror that reflects the true and diverse nature of our Father as Jesus did as He quoted *"If you have seen me; you have seen the Father"* also Jesus stated that *"I and the Father are one"* The second aspect of this scripture is that our Father resides and has estab-lished His throne in the heavens. **Revelation four** describes aspects of the place where our Father has set up His throne or seat of authority and government to rule over all creation and creatures. The writer John articulates with eloquence the majesty of the courts of our king and the worship of heaven. However, we will see that our Father wants to restore His kingdom from the heavens into the hearts of men and the systems of man; He wants a kingdom expansion in heaven and earth.

The Father, our Abba hath such an overflowing love towards mankind His fallen, lost children that He sent His own Son. The kind of love the Father has is one that is strong, constant, never-changing eternal affections. He does not have the sensual love commonly expressed between a married male and female in matrimony that can fluctuate. His love is not just a love of friendship or brotherly love expressed to siblings or peers. He expresses the Agapao (25) according to the *Lexical Aids* to the New Testament form of love. It indicates a direction of the will and finding one's joy in something. It is the God, unconditional, everlasting fixed form of love towards man.

Another translation is **Agape (26) meaning charity, benevolent love**. It is benevolence, 'it is shown by doing what the person loved desires but what the love giver feels the recipient needs. So the Father gave us His Son Jesus because our need for salvation is greater than any other need for existence. The Father gave us the gift of Jesus we needed Him or understood He is the source of our existence. Daddy gave us the best gift; He anticipated our insufficiencies, loved us eternally and made provisions for our eternal salvation and our earthly success. His love is unselfish, pure, and driven by the right motives to bless us. There are no hidden agendas of deception in our Father. His love does not require an applause or repayment. He just loves because He loves.

The Father gave His only begotten Son, His love was so intense that He was willing to give His best. There is power when believers are establish in Christ; the gift is available to all persons, whosoever. There is a salvaging of a person's life through the belief in the Father, in Jesus Christ.

How awesome! There is an everlasting protection and perseverance of the life in Christ. It is evident with the scriptures that our God and Father think about us with love and blessings; He intently yearns for the wholeness of every person.

Most importantly, He yearns for the salvation and restoration of man's dominion over the earth that was relinquished by Adam in the Garden of Eden. The writer of Peter describes the desires of the Father towards the eternal purpose, destiny and the salvation of man.

II Peter 3:9 *"The Lord is not slack concerning His promise, as some men count slackness; but is longsuf-fering to us-ward, not willing that any should perish but that all should come to repentance."*

Our papa the owner of heaven and earth is patient with His children. He is not desirous that any person perish due to sin. He does not want to see that destruction of the physical body of any person. He does not want the casting away of the mental degradation of His children. He is hurt by the very feelings of His children's infirmities. He is touched and even grieved when we His children endure the challenges of daily life. Every decision we make, papa is concerned about. Ultimately, He is mindful of the eternity of man.

He does not want anyone to live a life of suffering, denying His Son Jesus and spending everlasting existence in hell's flames.

John 3:16-18 *"For God so loved the world, that He gave His only begotten Son, that whosoever believeth in Him should not perish but have ever-lasting life."***(vs. 17)** *"For God sent not His Son into the world to condemn the world; but that the world through Him might be saved."*

(vs. 18) *"He that believeth on Him is not condemned: but He that believeth not is condemned already, because He hath not believed in the name of the only begotten Son of God."*

Jesus came to give life to the believers, a full complete purpose-filled existence. *Lexical Aids* to the New Testament describes to "the principle of life in the Spirit and Soul." Zoë is the nobler word, expressing all of the highest and best which Christ is and which He gives to the saints. Zoë life which the Father gives is the high-test form of life; it is the fullest and noble existence that Daddy gives. It is life as God has it, that which the Father has in Himself and which the Son manifested in the world.

The Father desires that we have a life above the struggling, barely existing, trying to make it through until Friday to engage in vain lifestyles. Daddy wants us to experience all the joys of individuality, family and covenantal relationships this life has to offer temporal but the eternal.

The Father's motive is driven by love and pure passion; He did not send Jesus into the world to bring an accusation against the world.

Humanity was already under a curse and did not deserve further weight of grief upon conscience and life. The Father wanted to establish and restore the relationship of man through Christ. Mankind would further restore the order of God in the earth. The love of God would re-order man's lost nature; His broken identity and secure His future in eternity. Man would rise up in the 'shalom' of God in this life and re-order the broken systems of humanity.

Chapter 10 End of Chapter Principles

∀ The Heavenly father is Holy and set apart as consecrated. He has no sin and cannot perform Sin.

∀ The Father is good, righteous and pure in thought, motive and intentions. His actions are always righteous.

∀ The Father is complete, whole and in Himself total. He is absolutely full and perfect in His charter, nature and development.

∀ Sons are commanded to be righteous, complete and whole like our heavenly Father.

∀ Our Father walks in a love that is above natural humanly feelings.

∀ He loved mankind so dearly that He came in the earth to salvage mankind through Jesus Christ.

∀ Jesus came to give Zoë life; which is the complete purpose-filled existence. The nobler and highest form of living.

Chapter 11

The Father gives Zoë life

!"

John 10:10 "The thief cometh not, but for to steal, and kill, and to destroy: I am come that they might have life, and that they might have it more abundantly."

*J*esus emphatically declares that one of His assigned purposes for coming to the earth was so that mankind would have this noble existence. The Father sent Jesus with a mission to die that His Sons would live.

Another writer states that Jesus gave up the abundance and majestic life with the father and with the agreement of the Father became poor to establish His Sons access to wealth and riches.

II **Corinthians 8:9** *"For ye know the grace of our Lord Jesus Christ, that, though He was rich, yet for your sakes He became poor, that ye through His poverty might be rich."*

What an amazing Father; He sacrificed His greatness of continuous worship and praises; crown of precious jewels and throne of authority to be born in a humble stable to establish our wealth.

This is similar in many ways to great earthly fathers who work long hard hours, giving us their own pleasures and even dreams to provide food and college fees so that their children can have a better life than they had.

The Father of glory was willing to give His children resources so that they can excel in this life.

I John 3:1 *"Behold what manner of love the Father hath bestowed upon us that we should be called the Sons of God: therefore the world knoweth us not, because it knew Him not."*

Zoë life from the Father

The Father is filled with love towards the lives of His children. In the dawn of the greatest period of mankind, an era of technological and medical breakthrough papa wants to give the gift of the Holy

Spirit and a superior life on earth. All across races, cultures, socio-economic and nations humans are in search of a people or grouping of people who exhibit peace in the midst of personal and international turmoil. Mankind is troubled with volatile financial and economic markets across the world. He is now in search of the truth in a creator. In fact many reading this book are still in search of purpose in life.

Yet in the rubble of torn lives the loving Father says and yearns to give His children life and a peacefully purpose-motivated shalom life. Life that is satisfied from the internal peace in Christ and not from the external achievement of career, business, and wealth accumulation or even family or intimate relations.

His Zoë life is the power life that He gives to enablement to overcome struggles of depression, lust, sexual perversion, homosexuality, fornication, lying, and deception. His Zoë life will melt away the lives of scars in His Sons.

It is the Father's good pleasure to give us:

🖋 The keys to His kingdom.

🖋 The kingdom implanted into the believer's life.

🖋 Kingdom rulership in the earth.

Luke 12:31-32 *"But rather seek ye the kingdom of God; and all these things shall be added unto you.*

(vs. 32) *"Fear not, little flock; for it is your Father's good pleasure to give you the Kingdom."*

Luke 22:29 *"And I appoint unto you a kingdom, as my Father hath appointed unto me…"*

The physician Luke records the profound revelation of the search and fulfillment of every individual. The pursuit of life as stated by the master teacher and life coach; Jesus is to seek after the knowledge of the Kingdom of God. Every individual is to look for the understanding and experience of the operation of the Heavenly Father's rulership both in heaven and in the earth. These transforming insights of man's identity can be fulfilled in the experience of the rule of Christ. Jesus prefaces these words with the meaning of man's existence. He warns of a life of anxiety and fear; and condemns an existence of only earth gratification.

Jesus warns that individuals should not be overwhelmed with solely the consumption of food, clothing and desires. He expresses that life is more valuable than the consumption of foods and the pursuits of clothing. Jesus condemns the destructive nature and habit of worrying about life. He defends the nature of the Father to provide for His children by comparing His provision for the birds. He articulates that the Father arrays the magnificent fields of flowers, lays down the grass hills and with His Word can cause them to wither away.

Jesus declares that mankind should not seek what they should eat or drink. His claim is that the children who are of the world; other nations consume their lives on these mate-rial. Jesus is not denying the obvious needs and reality of food, clothes and shelter for persons. However, the emphasis for effective existence should not hinge on these desires.

He emphatically express that the Heavenly Father knows that His Sons have needs while living in the Earth. The Heavenly Father has pre-knowledge of every general and specific need of His children. Including general necessities include the provision of food. The Father created our bodies and designed the organs to generate energy through food sources.

He realizes the energy for breathing, working and performing activities demand an energy source. He made the body with these mechanisms. He therefore is critically aware of the needs of the human body.

Jesus is reminding mankind that they are not petitioning the Father of an area He is not aware of. The request or passionate pursuit of food over the pursuit of the Father could be very insulting to the Lord. The product is telling the manufacturer what it needs to function when he already knows.

Jesus speaks that the Father knows that His children has these needs. Hence it can be presumed that the Father has made abundant provisions to supply every need. He has everything for our existence in the earth in store for His Sons. Hallelujah!

> **Luke 11:11** *"If a son shall ask bread of any of you that is a Father, will he give him a stone? Or if he asks a fish, will he for a fish give him a serpent?*

> **(vs. 12)** *"Or if he shall ask an egg, will he offer him a scorpion?*

> **(vs. 13)** *"If ye then, being evil, know how to give your children good gifts, how much more shall your heavenly Father give the Holy Spirit to them that ask him?"*

Jesus parallels a son asking an earthly father for food and receiving it. He states that an earthly father would not insult the child request and need for bread by giving a stone. The act of giving a stone demonstrates the lack of understanding of the child's requests, his needs and mocks his request. By not fulfilling the specific request of the child, the father could damage the relationship with His son; and cause mistrust of the son to the father. The father then <u>insults</u> the request of the son by giving him an object that is edible. The earthly father gives even animals that are potentially poisonous to His son. Jesus concludes that even the earthly father yearns to fulfill the request of the son to experience the joys of being a provider. The earthly father desires to observe the joys, excitement and gratification of the son with the provision of the earthly father.

Jesus states that earthly father knows how to give good gifts to their children. Therefore the Heavenly Father knows how to give the greatest gift to His Sons – the Holy Spirit. Within the package of the gift of the Holy Spirit resides the keys and direction to achieving everything material and spiritual need in the earth.

The Kingdom given by the Father:

I Corinthians 15:24-28 *"Then the end will come when He hands over the kingdom to God the Father after He has destroyed all dominion, authority and power."***(vs. 25)** *"For He must reign until He has put all His enemies under His feet."***(vs. 26)** *"The last enemy to be destroyed is death."*

I Corinthians 15: (vs. 27) *"For He hath put all things under His feet. But when He saith, all things are put under Him it is* *manifest that He is excepted, which did put all things under Him.*

(vs. 28) *"When He has done this, then the son Himself will be made subject to Him who put every-thing under Him, so that God may be all in all."*

Hebrews 2:9 *"But we see Jesus, who was made a little lower than the angels for the suffering of death, crowned with glory and honour; that He by the grace of God should taste death for every man."*

(vs. 10) *"For it became Him, for whom are all things, and by whom are all things, in bringing many sons unto glory, to make the captain of their salva-tion perfect through sufferings.*

(vs. 11) *"For both He that sanctifieth and they who are sanctified are all of one: for which cause He is not ashamed to call them brethren."*

(vs. 12*) "Saying, I will declare thy name unto my brethren, in the midst of the church will I sing praise unto thee."*

Ephesians 2:4 *"But God who is rich in mercy for His great love where with He loved us"*

(vs. 5) *"Even when we were dead in sins, hath quickened us together with Christ, (by grace ye are saved,).*

(vs. 6) *"And hath raised us up together, and made us sit together in heavenly places in Christ Jesus:*

(vs. 7) *"That is the ages to come He might show the exceeding riches of His grace in His kindness towards us through Christ Jesus."*

Sketched deep in time was a broken family relationship between God and His prized possession man. This distorted and disjointed body caused the world to be in a state of uproar and disorder. Mankind was no longer hearing the strong correction of the father nor His graceful encouragement. Instead, mankind was guided and governed by the rigidity of the laws of God and His appointed leaders. These selective leaders were teachers of the scripture, judges, kings, prophets and priests of the nation.

These officers were established to govern and rule the people of Israel into the purposes of God until such a time when the King Jesus would be their personal consultant, confident and friend.

Finally in the silence of God's prophetic voice in the earth arose the promise, the repairers of the gap, the son Jesus Christ. *"In the fullness of times, God sent forth His Son, born of a virgin."*

The time had fully come; God desired to call His Sons back to Himself, and His voice would now be heard. His sons would now have direct access to His warm embrace, His gentle words of comfort and correction.

Jesus was now here on earth to pull the fellowship of heaven with the sons of the earth to accomplish the will of the father in the earth. Jesus is described as the first begotten son of the Father. He was the first lineage God was about to create. Jesus was the new model for many after who would long for a life that was obedient to the will and purpose of the Father in the earth. He was the first of this lineage to reveal the understanding of what is truly meant to walk with the Father and to continually have communion with Him. He proved to the world that the Father longs for a more intimate relationship with man that surpasses the formalities of religion and ethical living.

He proved that the Father still talks to His people even in a time of colossal organizational, technological and human advancement. Jesus proved that God still crave for man to understand their true identity in the midst of strong cultural and ideological times in which they lived. Most importantly, Jesus exhibited through His life the initial purpose that the Father wishes to execute His love, mission, order and will through His precious Sons in the earth. *"To those that are led by the spirit, to them He gave the power to become the Sons of God."*

The *Lexical Aids* to the New Testament states that the word 'Power' or 'Exousia (Greek) portrays the following meanings:

1. Permission

2. Authority

3. Right

4. Liberty

The word '**Exousia**' also denotes '**executive power**'. It emphasizes justified, having the right to exercise power. Right and might to exercise power. Similarly, to any nation on earth, various positions on the legal system or judiciary signify authority. For example, a judge or police has the power, to execute justice or make transaction on behalf of that nation. Hence, if individuals violate any of the laws prescribed by the country. The police can use the authority conferred upon them to make an arrest on behalf of the state.

This very same principle applies to the legal authorization conferred upon the believer by a loving Father to represent His name and enforce His agenda in the earth. The believer has been given the full assurance that we can transact on behalf of Christ Jesus in the earth.

The disarray, disorder, abuse and destruction of millions of lives are simply a ripple effect of broken, misunderstood and absent identity in God the Father. The earth and mankind has lost seeing who they are. It reminds me of an illustration of peering into a looking glass. The more one looks into it the more the features of the face are observed. The blemish that was unnoticed a week prior can now be brilliantly observed. The colour of your eyes and skin completion is illuminated by looking into the mirror.

The more time spent in His presence the more we begin to see Him and understand Him. It is through this reflection that we begin to understand our true self. We begin to see areas that need to be developed and even seek for repentance and change. Maybe it is an attitude that needs correcting, a mindset that continues to hinder us and fear about our own insufficiencies are minded in the presence of the Lord.

Our strengths are reaffirmed; our gifts are clearly outlined and enjoyed. The purposes of our lives are made clear and precise in the presence of the Lord.

In the presence of the Lord, we are constantly made and formed into the very image of Christ. The word of God says *"We are as looking glass,"* we reflect His image and glory. Jesus came in the likeness, fullness and glory of the Father. He was the expressed image of the Father according to the book of Hebrews. He was in the splendor of the Father because of His continuous fellowship.

Jesus lived to fulfill a number of responsibilities including salvation, restoration and the shedding of His precious blood for the remission of sin.

However, there was another unspoken mission that has been overlooked through the centuries; Jesus came to restore the broken identity of man. He came to raise many sons in the exact same image of His life and to adopt those who were by nature outside of the family and covenant of God. According to Old Testament scripture only those who were direct lineage and offspring of Abraham and Israel had rights to have fellowship and blessings with God. However, God wanted to be an active father to all of humanity. He had to re-establish the true identity of humanity.

This identity is not from graduating from a prestigious university, neither descendants of a wealthy family, nor possession of talents and gifting. A true nature of a person is who you were created to be and fulfilled in Jesus.

I John 5:7-8 *"For there are three that bear record in heaven the <u>Father</u>, the <u>Word</u> and the Holy Ghost; these three are one."*

(vs. 8) *"And these are three that bear witness in earth, <u>the spirit</u> and <u>the water</u>. And the blood and these three agree in one."*

Another account **John 1:1-4; 14** *"In the beginning was the word, and the word was with God and the Word was God.*

(vs. 2) *"The same was in the beginning with God."*

(vs. 3) *"All things were made by Him; and without Him was not anything made that was made.*

(vs. 4) *"In Him was life, and the life was the light of men."*

(vs. 14*) "And the word was made flesh and dwelt among us, (and we beheld His glory, the glory as of the only begotten of the Father, full of grace and truth."*

The beloved John apostle wrote of the mystery of the (trichotomy) three in one God. This wonder will forever remain glorious that the Father, Jesus the Son and the Holy Spirit are one in nature, character, purpose and agreement. The above scripture outlines that in the Heavens that the Father, the Word and the Holy Spirit are one.

The *Lexical Aids* to the New Testament states that the definition of The Word (3056) is logos. **Logos** comes from the root word 'Lego' to speak by linking and knitting together connected discourse the inward thoughts and feelings of mind.

Logos expresses thought, intelligence and also which expresses it **"Logos** when it refers to discourse, it is regarded as the orderly linking and connecting together in corrected arrangement of words of the inward thoughts and feeling of the mind.

Hence Jesus is expressed as the word which is the personal manifestation, most only a part of the divine nature of the Father but expresses thought, nature and totality of all the ideas and words of the Father.

> **John 1:1-18** *"No man hath seen God at any time; the only begotten Son, which is in the bosom of the Father, He hath declared Him."*

These scriptures further clarify Jesus as the totality of the nature, thoughts, word and expressed image of the Father. This is especially so that mankind may briefly grasp the glory of the Father Jehovah. The writer states that from the beginning the 'Word' was and existed with the Father and the 'Word' was God.

It elaborates that the 'Word' was in the beginning with God and everything was made by the word. The 'Word' was the architect of all that existed in the universe. In the Word the Zoë life, the life that is complete, abundant and of the highest order when man accepts the word.

The writer then expresses in **John 1:14.** *"And the word was made flesh…"* the God of the universe who sat in the heavens ruling with royalty, sovereignty and power receiving glory due to Him came to earth. The word who formed the superstructure of the universe in the power of Hs glory; who spoke all that exist with His word of power stepped into an earthen body.

The Word who in **Genesis 1:28** decided to form the clay container of man to host the spirit of man himself, stood in the temporal dirt suit.

The word dwelt among humans in their form but expressed fully the nature and thoughts of God the Father.

The writer John states that *"men saw His glory and the glory was the glory of the only begotten of the Father."* As we recall the term **glory**, is not a mystical, deep and spooky concept. The word '**Glory**' means the <u>nature character,</u> <u>majesty, weight of wealth, splendor, riches and royalty.</u> Hence Jesus the word portrays the splendor of the Father's lifestyle and wealth. Hallelujah!!!

The term <u>only begotten</u> (3439), '**Mono-genes**' means **mono**-only and **gene** to form, to make. "**Monogenes**" means the only one of the family. Only John uses **Monogenes** to describe the relationship of Jesus to God the Father, presenting Him as the unique one, the only one (monos) of the family genos in the discussion of the relationship of the son to the father."

The 'genos' from which the word genes in 'monogenes' originally means stock, race and family.

The expression 'monogenes' as in genos Jesus Christ designated as the only one of the same stock in the relationship of the son to the Father. He is not to be understood as eternally born of the Father but only in His humanity was He born. Therefore, mono genes can be held as synonymous with the God-man. We gather the concept of the word is Jesus and Jesus is the only one of the kind that came from the Father. He is God in the flesh.

The prophetic writer Isaiah peered through times and down age to glimpse the glory of the Father in the person of Jesus Christ. He captured the fullness of Jesus, His nature, His assignment, purpose and eternal plan to establish His Kingdom.

> **Isaiah 9:6-7** *"For unto us a Child is born, unto us a son is given and the government shall be upon His shoulder and His name shall be called wonderful Counseller, The mighty God, The everlasting Father, The Prince of Peace.*
>
> **(vs. 7)** *"Of the increase of His government and peace there shall be no end, upon the throne of David, and upon His Kingdom, to order it and to establish it with judgment and with justice from henceforth even forever. The zeal of the Lord of will perform this."*

Jesus the Word is described prophetically by Isaiah as the above titles only given to God the Father. He describes Jesus as the Wonderful and the mighty God! Praise God. This prophetic writer describes that this child born would be called by the name ascribe only to the Heavenly Father that is "the everlasting Father."

> **Isaiah 7:14** *"Therefore the Lord Himself shall give you a sign; behold, a virgin shall conceive, and bear a son, and shall call His name Immanuel."*

Matthew 1:18 *"Now the birth of Jesus Christ was on this wise: where as His mother Mary was espoused to Joseph, before they came together, she was found with child of the Holy Ghost."*

(vs. 20) *"But while he thought on these things behold, the angel of the Lord appeared unto him in a dream, saying Joseph, thou son of David, fear not to take unto thee Mary thy wife for that which is conceived in her is of the Holy Spirit."***(vs. 21)** *"And she shall bring forth a son, and thou shalt call His name JESUS: for He shall serve His people from their sins."*

Matthew 1: (vs. 23) *"Behold a virgin shall be with child, and shall bring forth a son, and they shall call his name Emmanuel, which being interpreted is God with us."***(vs.25)** *"And knew her not till she had brought forth her firstborn son: and he called His name Jesus."*

The apostle Matthew began his writing with the gene-alogy of Mary and Joseph the parental covering for Jesus. Joseph, however, was not the natural father of Jesus but acted as a spiritual Father for <u>Jesus</u>. Joseph receives a confirmation for his uncertain heart concerning the emasculate conception of Jesus. An angel declared that Jesus was the result of the Holy Spirits conception and creative powers. The angels also expressed instructionally that the son's name should be called Jesus.

The definition of the name of **Jesus** is powerful to the nature, purpose and power of Sonship in Jehovah. As this book will make reference to is the proceeding chapters, Jesus examplified the life of a true Son of God.

Jesus Christ is significant to the purpose of the Father to establish His Kingdom in the earth through the Sons. Jesus' life, words, authority and purpose represents that He is the authentic son of God. Jesus is referred to in scripture from the original text as '**Huios',** from the Greek means **"The Son."** He was not just any creation of God.

He is the actual person, the very essence and expressed thoughts of the Father within the confines of human finite understanding.

Jesus' life is very significant to the present believer as He lived not just to establish the law and the new covenant but to "...call many Sons." He came to establish a new lineage of believers who fellowship with God in a relationship. Adam was stated as the first man and Jesus is known as the second Adam. Like Adam, Jesus has no earthly Father but was directly fathered only by the spirit of God.

Scientifically, the Father determines the blood production and type of its offspring. Hence, both Adam in the pre-fallen state and Jesus were sons with a pure line or genetic make-up. They were not formed in contamination or genes of a sinful nature. Adam was born sinless but was lead by the spirit-led life and not from the desires of fleshly appetites.

Adam fell to rebellion and disobedience in the Garden of Eden and not only died a spiritual death but later a physical death. Adam by deception gave his Kingdom dominion and sovereign rule giving the Father command to have dominion over to earth to Satan.

Genesis 2:16 *"And the Lord God commanded the man saying of every tree of the garden thou mayest freely eat:"*

(vs. 17) *"But of the tree of knowledge of good and evil, thou shalt not eat of it: for in the day that thou eatest there of thou shalt die."*

The above scriptures outline the instruction of the Lord to Adam, the Father of all humans throughout the ages. Adam was commanded not to eat the fruit and the consequences were explained by the Father.

Genesis 3:6 *"And when the woman saw that tree was good for food, and that it was pleasant to the eyes, and a tree to be desired to make one wise, she took of the fruit thereof, and did eat, and gave also unto her husband with her; and he did eat."*

The verse outlines the deception of the serpent to the mother of all humans Eve. She was beguiled by the lies of the serpent and noted the fruit to be luring to her eyes. Eve gave Adam the fruit and He eats. He activated the process and penalty of sin in their lives. They both started the deterioration of death and the relinquishing of dominion authority to Satan.

Jesus therefore is vital to the restoration, redemption, re-establishment of the Sons of God to relationship with the Father. He came to establish a new lineage of Sons, those who will walk with the Father like Adam in His pre- fallen state.

Jesus from *Vine's Complete Expository Dictionary* of Old and New Testament word defined as the **Greek Ieseus (**2424) which is a translation of the Hebrew "**Joshua**" meaning **"Jehovah is Salvation"** and **"the Saviour."** It was given to the son of God incarnation as His personal name, in obedience to the command of an angel to Joseph. The name Jesus has a prophetic declaration of His assignment from His glorious name.

Jesus was called by God to restore or place man back into His position of righteous government and authority under the sovereign partnership with Jehovah God.

The Father yearns for the restoration of His Sons. This word 'Son' from the original language and text has two words. One word definition is '**Tekna,'** which connotes a young child in reference to scripture; it suggests that all of humanity is the offspring or creation of God. However, the second term of **Huios** refers to a mature son.

The word 'son' is not a term of gender but one of relationship. It indicates position of fellowship and of God. These qualities lead to the maturity of a believer to that of a saint who has access and authority to conduct the will of God in the earth. This position of sonship crosses all manmade boundaries. It supervenes the ethnic, racial and socioeconomic limitations that have marginalize the believers from walking in their God given authority.

Sonship has unlimited potential to propel a believer unto every promise and blessing that the heavenly Father has in store through Jesus Christ.

Jesus, the firstborn son became the one through whom came many sons to the Father. Through Jesus the lost Sons will learn the inheritance God has left. The world is introduced to the Royal family that humanity can be adopted into the kingly family. We are children of the King.

Through intimately and intricately studying the life and ministry of Jesus the Holy Spirit will begin to gently whisper the mysteries of Jesus Christ. The life of those who seek restored fellowship with the Father will be opened to the process of daily development that God desires. Jesus makes many profound and bold claims that He and the Heavenly Father were one being.

> **John 17:11** *"And now I am no more in the world, but these are in the world and I come to thee. Holy Father, keep through thine own name those whom thou hast given me that they may be one as we are."*

> **John 17:21** *"That they all may be one, as thou, Father, art in me, and I in thee, that they also may be one in us: that the world may believe that thou hast sent me."* **(vs. 22)** *"And the glory which thou gavest me I have given them; that they may be one, even as we are one:"*

> **John 17:(vs. 23)** *"I in them, and thou in me, that they may be made perfect in one; and that the world may know that thou hast sent me, and hast loved them, as thou hast loved me."*

(vs. 24) *"Father I will that they also whom thou hast given me He with me where I am; that they may behold my glory, which thou hast given me for thou lovedst me before the foundation of the world."*

Our Lord Jesus in His intercessory prayer of **John 17** admonishes the Heavenly Father to restore Him to His former place of authority and majesty. He wanted to reclaim His place in the Heavenlies as supreme Lord and shed the earthen vessel. His assignment of relationship, restoration and re-establishing the kingdom of the Father back to the executives in the earth was complete. Jesus had made all provisions and was embarking in the proceeding chapters to be the sacrificial lamb that would be slain so that man would be reconnected to the Father through Jesus' blood. Many who would believe would be given the power to become matured sons of God.

Jesus in a narrative manner communes with the Father, interceded for the Sons of God who walked with Him but also those who would be adopted into the Family of God throughout the ages. Jesus also reveals the mystery of our God; His ones with the Father. He states *"...that they may be one as we are one."* **John 17:11**

John 17 (vs. 21) *"That they all may be one as thou, Father, art in me; and I in thee that* *they also may be one in us: that the world may believe that thou hast sent me."***(vs. 22)*** "...that they may be one, even as we are one."*

Other emphatic claims of His lordship are in **John 10:30** *"I and my Father are one." And in* **John 10:38** *"But if I do through ye believe not me, believe the works: that ye may know, and believe; that the Father is in me, and I in Him."*

Praise God! Jesus is Lord of everything. Paul the apostle in His writing to the believers and followers of Christ in Phillip reiterates the true identity of Jesus. Paul also power-fully utters the purpose and authority of Jesus over death, sin and every other name.

Philippians 2:5 *"Let this mind be in you, which was in also in Christ Jesus.*

(vs. 6) *"Who being in the form of God, thought it not robbery to be equal with God:* **(vs. 7)** *"But made Himself of no reputation and took upon Him the form of a servant, and was made in the likeness of men:*

Philippians (vs. 8) *"And being found in fashion as a man He humbled Himself,* *and became obedient unto death, even the death of the cross."*

(vs. 9) *Wherefore God also hath highly exalted Him, and given Him a name which is above every other name:***(vs. 10)** *"That at the name of Jesus every knee should bow, of things in heaven, and things in earth and things under the earth;***(vs. 11)** *"And that every tongue should confess that Jesus Christ is Lord, to the glory of God the Father."*

This passage lays the foundation of Jesus being the nature and essence of the Heavenly Father. It articulates magnificently the process in which the Father wrapped Himself unassumingly in the suit of a baby in Mary's womb. He was driven by the passion into cross of death. His name is now highly exalted and glorified above every name of demons, diseases, conditions, circumstances and every enemy of the King's rule in our lives. Halleluiah! His name also has authority in the heaven invisible and spheres through out the universe

Chapter 11 End of Chapter Principles

∀ Jesus came to give an abundant life or nobler, highest form of human existence.

∀ Jesus left the majesty of heaven's royalty to become poor to give sons His royal nature and access.

∀ The Father appointed or conferred kingdom authority to His Sons.

∀ Jesus express that man's desire should be for the Kingdom and not for material possession.

∀ The Father knows the needs of His children but wants them to seek diligently their lost dominion in the Kingdom.

∀ The Kingdom authority has been delegated to faithful sons in the earth.

∀ The Spirit gives mankind the potential through obedience to become Sons of God.

∀ Jesus is the word of God the father.

∀ **Jesus is the Father warmed in humanly form for the purpose of restoring mankind and being an eternal intercessor.**

∀ **Jesus is the Son of God; the only begotten of the Heavenly Father.**

∀ **Jesus is vital to the restoration, redemption, re-estab-lishment of the Sons of God to relationship with the Father.**

Chapter 12

Jesus the anointed King

!"

Colossian 1:15-18 "Who is the image of the invisible God, the firstborn of every creature:

(vs. 16) "For by Him were all things created that are in heaven and that are in earth, visible and invis-ible, whether they be thrones or dominions or prin-cipalities or powers: all things were created by Him and for Him:

(vs. 17) "And He is before all things and by Him all things consist."

(vs. 18) "And He is the head of the body, the church: who is the beginning the firstborn for the dead that in all things He might have the preeminence.

(vs. 19) "For it pleased the Father that in Him should all fullness dwell;"

*P*aul expresses the mysteries of Jesus in His book to the followers at Colosse. He declares that Jesus is the image of the Heavenly Father. The word image portrays the concept of resemblance. The *Lexical Aids* to the New Testament gives the Greek meaning of **image as:**

🖊 To be like

🖊 Resemble

'Eikon', image, always assumes a prototype, that which it not merely resembles, but from which it is drawn. Thus the reflection of the sun on the water is **'Eikon'**.

Another Greek word used for 'image' is character presented in

> **Hebrews 1:2** *"Hath in these last days spoken unto us by His son, whom He hath appointed heir of all things by whom also He made the worlds.*
>
> **(vs. 3)** *"Who being the brightness of His glory and the <u>express image</u> of His person and upholding all things by the word of His power, when He had by Himself purged our sins, sat down on the right hand of the majesty on high."*

Lexical Aids states that character signifies the image impressed as corresponding with the original or pattern. On account of this idea of close resemblance it has for its synonym **mumema** (Greek), **imitation, anything imitated a copy.**

Jesus is the essence of the Father in nature character and relationship. He is the prototype, the firstborn of all creation. Another vital title in assisting us discovers this Lord Jesus and in establishing our pattern of life with the heavenly father is the word firstborn. This word firstborn comes from **Prototokos** from **protos (first) and tikto (5088)** meaning to bear or bring forth. *Lexical Aids* accounts that Jesus "He is called the first-begotten or the firstborn of the whole creation, in that He existed before all things, and everything both in heaven and earth were created by Him."

Christ is also called in **Hebrews 1:6** "**Prototokos nekton nekton**" meaning the firstborn or first begotten from the dead in regard to His being the first who rose from the dead, no more to die; being the first to arise to an *"immortal an incorruptible life."* He is also referred to the firstborn among brethren, both in holiness and glory.

Jesus in the book of **Colossians 1** is defined as the creator of all things; and the one with whom all things were created for.

All government systems and authorities are subdued and subjected to His kingdom. This means governments, nations, religions and also satanic systems of government are under the rulership of His creative power.

Paul expresses the heavenly Father and Jesus' relation-ship intricately presented in the book of Ephesians.

> **Ephesians 1:19** *"And what is the exceeding great-ness of His power to us-ward who believe, according to His mighty power,*
>
> **(vs. 20)** *"Which He wrought in Christ when He raised Him from the dead, and set Him at His own right hand in the heavenly places,*
>
> **(vs. 21)** *"Far above all principalities, and power, and <u>might</u> and <u>dominion</u> and every name that is named, not only in this world, but also in that which is to come:*
>
> **(vs. 22)** *"And hath put all things under His feet, and gave Him to be the head over all things to the church,* **(vs. 23)** *"Which is His body the fullness of Him that filleth all in all."*

Power in the name

Matthew 1:21 *"And she shall bring forth a son, and thou shalt call His name JESUS: for He shall save His people from their sins."*

The Father in all His divine wisdom and strategic purpose, stepped into the realm of earth, choose a title to express His purpose. Solomon the writer expressed that a good name is valued more than precious stones and jewels. The Father did that in the name of Jesus. The name of Jesus as seen in the earlier text of **Philippians 2:10** are given above every other name in all realms in heaven and earth. His name demands respect, honour and obedience. What then is so significant about the name of Jesus?

The name 'Jesus' means 'Saviour' and expresses His office and authority functions. The word 'name' implies and encaptures the authority, character, rank, majesty, power, excellence.

The description of "Christ" is loaded with the office and redemptive purpose of Jesus. **Jesus Christ** signifies the person of the heavenly Father; the assignments of salvation and restoration of the dominion position of all sons.

Christ came to re-establish the lineage of spiritual sons, and the gifting of the Holy Spirit back into the lives of His Sons. Christ became the second Adam, after the first Adam lost by delegation the kingdom of the earth to Satan in the Garden of Eden.

Jesus Christ the first begotten of the Father outlines through His life the pattern of divine fellowship with the Father and the power that is released from the connection with daddy.

The word Christ comes from the Greek **'Christos'** (5547**) means to anoint, the anointed One. It is** translated in the Hebrew as 'Messiah'. It denotes a term applied to the priests who were anointed with the holy oil, particularly the high priest. Jesus was given the enablement to carry the office of all His function by the anointing or smearing of the Holy Spirit. He was consecrated, set apart unto holiness and equipped with the capacity to function in the purpose of the Father.

> **Luke 4:16-19** *"And He came to Nazareth, where He had been brought up: and, as His custom was, He went into the synagogue on the Sabbath day, and stood up for to read.'*
>
> **(vs. 17)** *"And there was delivered unto Him the book of the prophet Isaiah. And when He had opened the book, He found the place where it was written,*

(vs. 18) *"The spirit of the Lord is upon me, because He hath anointed me to preach the gospel to the poor; He hath sent me to heal the brokenhearted, to preach deliverance to the captives and recovering of sight to the blind to set at liberty them that are bruised,*

(vs. 19) *"To preach the acceptable year of the Lord."*

The physician Luke gives an account of the profound self-declaration of Jesus Christ to humanity. He read a scroll given to Him on a divine day in which the text outlines specifically His assignment and purpose in the earth. With tremendous conviction and authority, Jesus declared that He was the fulfillment of the text, the word written by the prophetic writer Isaiah. Jesus claimed the scriptures and strategically emphasized to such power that the listeners knew that He internalized the scripture and projected into the listeners. Praise God!!

Jesus came to give life

John 6:40 *"And this is the will of Him that sent me, that every one which seeth the Son and believeth on Him, may have* *everlasting life: and I will raise Him up at the last day."*

(vs. 47) *"Verily, verily, I say unto you, he that believeth on me hath everlasting life."*

(vs. 48) *"I am that bread of life."*

(vs. 51) *"I am the living bread which came down from heaven: if any man eat of this bread, He shall live forever: and the bread that I will give is my flesh, which I will give for the life of the world."*

John 10:9 *"I am the door: by me if any man enters in, he shall be saved, and shall go in and out and find pasture.*

(vs. 10) *"The thief cometh not, but for to steal, and to kill, and to destroy: I am come that they might have life and it abundantly."*

Jesus Christ expresses that through faith in Him and obedience to His laws; fallen Sons can be restored to Kingdom living. He is the sacrifice paid by His death and crushing of His body for access to the Father. Jesus offers to life Greek 'Zoë' life for all persons. The Zoë life is the kingdom living in which Sons of God lives above the nature of son, limitations of cultural and national identities and can fulfill the abundance the

Father intended. The Father intended for His children to walk in continuous health, financial abundance and 'shalom.' From the earlier text, the Hebrews word 'shalom' expresses a life of completeness, wholeness, harmony in every aspect of life, wealth, health, happiness and inner joy in every situation. It is the God kind of life Adam walked in before the fall, where there was abundance, dominion and wealth by inheritance and not hard non-productive over-working. Everything Adam had brought forth Harvest returns increase, abundance before His fall to rebellion.

Adam had full dominion over His environment, naming authority over every creature; the covering of God's presence and open channels to commune with the Father.

Jesus access granted!!

The Father through Jesus Christ has given us the security code to the vault of heavens store. Jesus made it possible to avail salvation; direct access to the heavenly Father, restore identity and wisdom. Jesus' esteem transfer of inheritance was made through His blood.

> **Hebrew 9:14** *"How much more shall the blood of Christ, who through the eternal spirit offered Himself without spot to God, purge your conscience from dead works to serve the living God?*

(vs. 15) *"And for this cause He is the mediator of the New Testament, that by means of death, for the redemption of the transgressions that were under the first testament they which are called might receive the promise of the <u>eternal inheritance</u>."*

(vs. 22) *"And almost all things are by the law purged with blood; and without shedding of blood is no remission."*

Hebrews 10:10 *"By the will we are sanctified through the offering of the body of Jesus Christ once for all."*

The innocent shed blood of Jesus has made the standard by which 'bastard' children can be made Sons. Through the crucifixion of Jesus, there is remission or forgiveness of violation to the laws of God. The Father honours the blood of Jesus and accepts mankind to receive that salvation of the Lord.

The word salvation gets its original meaning from the Greek **'soteria'** (4991) from **'sozo'** (4982) to save in the *Lexical Aids* to the New Testament

'Sozo' expresses the meaning of:

- Salvation relating to material and temporary deliver-ance from danger, sufferings and sickness. It represents preservation.

- The spiritual and eternal salvation granted immediately by God to those who believe on Christ.

- The present experience of God's power to deliver from the bondage of sin.

Hebrews 10:19 *"Having therefore, brethren bold-ness to enter into the holiest by the blood of Jesus*

(vs. 20) *"By a new and living way, which he hath consecrated for us through the veil, that is to say His flesh;*

(vs. 21) *"And having a high priest over the house of God;"*

(vs. 22) *Let us draw near with a true heart in full assurance of faith, having our hearts sprinkled from an evil conscience and our bodies washed with pure water."*

The writer of Hebrews admonishes and clarifies that the son of God with faith in Jesus Christ should approach the Father boldly. The blood shed by Jesus is the key to unlocking the doors into the holy inner courts where the Father resides. The boldness should arise from an understanding of the completed assignment of Jesus Christ. The tenacity should spring from an illumination that there is a right for the sons of God to enter His presence through Jesus.

The confidence a son should enter into the request room of the Father is through the inheritance and adoption of our spirit to our Father. Jesus' sacrifice should stir the zeal of our confidence and not by what humanity has accomplished. Jesus has been set apart unto the holy purpose of allowing sons to be accepted to praise and petition in the inner courts, praise God. Sons can petition for salvation, forgiveness, health, wealth and stand confident that through Jesus the Father hears our request. Sons can directly enter into His gates with thanksgiving and into His courts with praise. They have precious moments where through worship, the blood of Christ and access to meet with the King of all the earth. Man can now enter into ultimate fellowship with daddy to share the dreams and receive His hearts desires. They can hear the passion of the Father and partner with His eternal plan to establish His glorious kingdom in the earth.

Hebrews 12:24 *"And to Jesus the mediator of the new covenant and to the blood of sprinkling."*

Jesus access granted:

John 6:44 *"No man can come to me except the Father which hath sent me draw him: and I will raise him up at the last day."*

(vs. 65) *"And he said, therefore said I unto you that no man can come unto me except it were given unto him of my father."*

The writer of John captures the Father's purpose in Jesus Christ. Jesus states that there is a drawing of man's spirit to the revelation of Jesus' assignment. He emphatically declares that it is the Heavenly Father that attracts man towards The Son, Jesus Christ. The Father opens the eyes of man's understanding to receive Jesus as the express image of the Father and the mandate of the Kingdom expansion in the earth.

The Father gives granted access to the partnership with Jesus and His ministry. The Father provides, shares in the companies business for man but they must go to the CEO of the company.

The Father represents the owner of the company and all its assets. He assigns Jesus as the Chief Executive Officer who oversees the company on the owner's behalf. The Holy Spirit who the Father also gives in Jesus' name is the legal advisor, advocate and auditor. The Father gives the Holy Spirit on behalf of the sons. Through partnership the earth and arenas of influence will be subjected to the laws of Jesus to His glory!!

Jesus came from the Father

John 16:25-28 *"These things have I spoken unto you in proverbs: but the time cometh, when I shall no more speak unto you in proverbs, but I shall show you plainly of the Father."*

(vs. 26) *"At the day ye shall ask in my name: and I say not unto you, that I will pray the Father for you.*

(vs. 27) *"For the Father Himself loveth you, because ye have loved me and have believed that I came out from God."*

(vs. 28) *"I came forth from the Father, and am come into the world: again I leave the world, and go to the Father."*

Jesus explains that His Sons will request access in His name. His name portrays a person's character, reputation, influence and authority. Jesus declares the love of the Father and His out poured love on His Sons because of their love for Him. There is a stream of love that issues from the Father on acceptance of the Son Jesus Christ. Jesus declares that a token of favour will flow towards those who receive that He came from, out of the Heavenly Father.

Jesus clarifies the answer to any uncertainty about His purpose and character. Jesus came from the Father to express His nature love and restorative plan for man. Jesus declared that He will return to the Father. He is fixed that the assignment to restore and re-establish the Kingdom of His Father and co-heir with man in the earth. Praise God.

Jesus and the Father are one

John 14:8 *"Phillip saith unto Him Lord, show us the Father, and it sufficeth us.*

(vs. 9) *"Jesus saith unto him, have I been so long time with you and yet hast thou not known me Philip? He that hath seen me hath seen the Father and how sayest thou their, show us the Father?*

(vs. 10) *Believest thou not that I am in the Father, and the Father in me? The words that I speak unto you I speak not of myself: but the Father that dwelleth in me he doth the works.*

(vs. 11) *"Believe me that I am in the Father, and the Father in me: who else believe me for the very works sake."*

Jesus will ask for the Father's Praise

John 14:13 *"And whatsoever ye shall ask in my name, that will I do that the Father may be glorified in the Son.*

(vs. 14) *"If ye shall ask anything in my name, I will do it."*

Jesus prays for the Holy Spirit

John 14:16 *"And I will pray the Father, and he shall give another comforter, that he may abide with you forever."*

John 14:26 *"But the comforter, which is the Holy Ghost, whom the Father will send in my name, he shall teach you all things, and bring all things to your remembrance, whatsoever I have said unto you."*

Jesus and the Love Connection

John 15:9 *"As the Father hath loved me, so have I loved you: continue ye in my love."*

(vs. 10) *"If ye keep my commandments, ye shall abide in my love; even as I have kept my Father's commandments, and abide in His love."*

Jesus gives all to His friends:

John 15:13 *"Greater love hath no man than this that a man lay down his life for his friends."*

(vs. 14) *"Ye are my friends, if ye do whatsoever I command you."*

(vs. 15) *"Henceforth I call you not servants; for servant knoweth mot what his Lord Doeth: but I have called you friends; for all things that I have heard of my Father I have made known unto you."*

(vs. 16) *"Ye have not chosen, me but I have chosen you and ordained you, that ye should go and bring forth fruits, and that your fruit should remain: that whatsoever ye shall ask of the Father in my name, he may give it you."*

John 16:23 *"And in the day ye shall ask me nothing verily, verily, I say unto you, whatsoever ye shall ask the Father in my name, he will give it you."*

(vs. 24) *"Hitherto have ye asked nothing in my name: ask ye shall receive, that your joy may be full."*

John 8:18 *"I am one that bear witness of myself, and the Father that sent me bearth witness of me."*

(vs. 19) *"Then, said they unto him, where is thy Father? Jesus answered, Ye neither know me, nor my Father: if ye had known me, ye should have known my Father also.*

Jesus does only what the Father speaks to Him:

John 8:27-29 *"They understood not that he spake to them of the Father."*

(vs. 28) *Then said Jesus unto them, when ye have lifted up the Son of man, then shall ye know that I am he and that I do nothing of myself but as my Father hath taught me, he speak these things"*

(vs. 29) *"And He that sent me is with me: the Father hath not left me alone; for I do always those things that please Him."*

The Father honours Jesus

John 8:52 *"Then said the Jesus unto him, now we know that thou hast a devil.*

Abraham is dead, and the prophets; and thou sayest if a man keep my saying, he shall never taste of death."

(vs. 54) *"Jesus answered, if I honour myself, my honour is nothing: it is my Father that honoreth me; of whom ye say, that he is your God.*

(vs. 55) *"Yet ye have not known him; but I know him: and I should say I know him not, I shall be a liar like unto you: but I know him, and keep his saying."*

Jesus lay down His life for the Father and His Children

John 10:17 *"Therefore doth my Father love me, because I lay down my life, that I might take it again."*

(vs. 18) *"No man taketh it from me but I lay it down of myself. I have power to lay it down and I have power to take it again. This commandment have I received of my Father."*

John 10:30 *"I and my Father are one."*

Jesus is the way to the Father

John 14:6 *"Jesus saith unto him, I am the way, the truth, and the life: no man cometh unto the Father but by me."*

(vs. 7) *"If ye had known me ye should have known my Father also, and from hence forth ye know him, and have seen him."*

John 5:19 *"There answered Jesus and said unto them, verily, verily I say unto you, The Son can do nothing of Himself; but what He seeth the Father do: for what things soever He doeth, these also doeth the Son likewise."*

(vs. 20) *"For the Father loveth the Son, and showeth him all things that himself doeth: and he will show him greater works than these that ye may marvel."*

(vs. 21) *"For as the Father rises up the death, and quickened whom he will."*

(vs. 22) *"For the Father judged no man, but hath committed all judgment unto the son:*

(vs. 23) *"That all men should honour the Son even as they honour the Father; He* that honoureth not the Son honoureth not the Father which hath sent him;

(vs. 26) *"For is the Father hath life in himself; so hath he given to son to have life in himself;*

(vs. 27) *"And hath given him authority to execute judgment also, because he is the son of man."*

Jesus comes in the Father's name

John 5:43 *"I am come in my Father's name, and ye receive me not: if another shall come in my Fathers name, and ye receive me not: if another shall come in his own name, him ye will receive."*

Jesus sent from Heaven. **(John 6:38-41)**

Jesus our Lord

I John 5:7-8 *"For there are three that bear record in heaven the <u>Father</u>, the <u>word</u> and the <u>Holy Ghost</u>. These three are one."*

(vs. 8) *"And these are three that bear witness in earth, the spirit and the water and the blood: and these three agree in one."*

John 1:1 *"In the beginning was the Word, and the Word was with God, and the Word was God."*

(vs. 2) *"The same was in the beginning with God."*

(vs. 3) *"All things were made by Him; and without Him was not any thing made that was made.*

(vs. 4) *"In Him was life; and the life was the light of men."*

John 1:14 "*And the Word was made flesh and dwelt among us, (and we beheld His glory, the glory as of the only begotten of the Father), full of grace and truth."*

Jesus declares the Father:

John 1:18 *"No man hath seen God at anytime; the only begotten Son, which is in the bosom of the Father, he hath declared him."*

I John 4:2 *"Hereby know ye the spirit of God: every spirit that confesseth that Jesus Christ is come in the flesh is of God:*

(vs. 3) *And every spirit that confesseth not that Jesus Christ is come in the flesh is not of God: and this is the spirit of God: and this is the spirit of anti-christ, whereof ye have heard that it should come; and ever now already is it in the world.*

(Vs. 9) *"In this was manifested the love of God toward us, because that God sent His only begotten Son unto the world that we might live through Him."*

(vs. 10) *"Herein love, not that we loved God, but that He loved us and sent His son to be propitiation for sins."*

(vs. 14) *"And we have seen and do testify that the Father sent the Son to be the Saviour of the world."* **(vs. 15)** *"Whatsoever shall confess that Jesus is the Son of God, God dwelleth in him, and he in God."*

I John 5:10 *"He that believeth on the Son of God hath the witness in himself: he that believeth not God hath made him a liar; because he believeth not the record that God gave of His Son.*

(vs. 11) *"And this is the record that God hath given to us eternal life, and this life is in his Son."*

(vs. 12) *"He that hath the Son hath life: and he that hath not the Son of God hath not life."*

(vs. 13) *"These things have I written unto you that believe on the name of the Son of God; that ye have eternal life and that ye may believe on the name of the Son of God."*

Jesus a Son:

Jesus according to scripture and original Greek transla-tion was always referred to as 'Son'. He was not a child of God but was expressed as the 'Son' indicating His intimate fellowship and inseparable nature to the Heavenly Father.

In the account of Jesus' humanly birth He is never desig-nated as *'teknon'* meaning to target or, bear child) or 'teknon Theou', a child of God but always *'ho Huios'* 'the Son' or the 'Son of man'.

The word 'teknon' is related to another Greek term *tikto* (5088) meaning to beget or bear child. It is also used in both the natural and figurative senses giving prominence to the fact of birth, whereas *Huios* (5207), son in a generic sense, stresses the dignity and character

154

of the relationship" (*Lexical Aids* to the New Testament).Jesus throughout the scripture expressed emphatically His intimacy and oneness with the Heavenly Father. He expressed Himself as being equal with the father; concern with fulfilling the father's will and making known the Father to the new line of Sons.

> **John 5:19** *"Then answered Jesus and said unto them, verily verily, I say unto you, The Son can do nothing of himself, but what he seeth the Father do: for what things soever he doeth, these also doeth the Son likewise***(vs. 23)** *"That all men should honour the son, even as they honour the Father. He that honoreth not the Son honoreth not the Father which hath sent him."*

> **John 10:30** *"I and my Father are one.*

The scriptures reveal the Sonship of Jesus. He was not merely an immature creation of the Father but a developed Son who knew the purpose and assignment of the Father in His life. He was interwoven with the heart beat of the Father. He was consumed with the will and agenda of the Father. His life stream that flowed through His veins was the expansion of the Kingdom through the Sons of God in the earth.

In the book *The Case for Christ* by Lee Strobel, Ben Witherington III, (PhD) states, pg. 133- "If He

(Jesus) had simply announced, 'Hi folks; I'm Yahweh,' because the Jews of His day didn't have any concept of the Trinity. They only knew of God the Father-whom they called Yahweh-and not God the son or God the Holy Spirit." So if someone were to say "He was God, that wouldn't have made any sense to them and would have been seen as a clear-cut blasphemy. And it would have been counterproductive to Jesus in His efforts to get people to listen to His message. In addition to employing the "Amen phrase in His teaching, Jesus used term "Abba" when He was relating to God. "What does that tell us about what He thought about Himself?" I asked.

'Abba' connotes intimacy in a relationship between a child and his father," Witherington explained. Interestingly, it's also the term disciples used for a beloved teacher in early Judaism. But Jesus used it of God.

In the context in which Jesus operated, it was customary for Jews to work around having to say the name of God. His name was the most holy word you could speak, and they even feared mispronounciating it. If they were going to address God, they might say something like, 'The Holy One, blessed is He,' but they were not going to use His personal name. And Abba is a personal term… it implies that Jesus had a degree of intimacy with God that is unlike anything in Judaism of His day." "…Jesus is saying that only through having a rela-tionship with He does this kind of prayer language-this kind of Abba relationship with God become possible."

> **John 14:5** *"Thomas said unto Him, Lord, we know not whither thou goest and how can we know the way?'*

> **(vs. 6)** *"Jesus saith unto him, I am the way, the truth, and the life: no man cometh unto the Father, but by me."*

> **(vs. 7)** *"If ye had known me, ye should have known my Father also: and from henceforth ye know Him, and have seen Him."*

> **(vs. 8)** *"Philip saith unto Him, Lord, show us the Father, and it sufficeth us.*

> **(vs. 9)** *"Jesus saith unto him, have I been so long time with you, and yet hast thou not known me, Philip? He that hath seen me hath seen the Father; and how sayest thou them, show us the Father?*

> **(vs. 10)** *Believest thou not that I am in the Father, and the Father in me? That words that I speak unto you I speak not of myself: but the Father that dwelleth in me, He doeth the works."*

(vs. 11) *"Believe me that I am in the Father, and the Father in me: or else believe me for the very works sake."*

(vs. 12) *"Verily, verily, I say unto you He that believeth on me, the works that I do shall he do also and greater works than these shall he do; because I go unto my Father."*

Jesus declares that His life, work, miracles and ministry express the Father's heart. He declares that by following His words, commandments and purposeful actions, one can vividly understand the Father. Jesus declares Himself to be equal with the Heavenly Father. He is the Son, the earthly representative of the image of God. He was driven by the Holy Spirit; He was matured to the assignment and obedient to the will of the Father. Jesus' exemplary life was above the daily self-gratifications of food, fame and riches. His maturity above being a child of God ('teknon') to Huios conformed Him to diligently striving for fulfillment of the Father's purpose.

He was passionate about pleasing the Father, while in the humanly body. His mission was to glorify the Father in His life and work in the earth. His fellowship with the Father in prayer and submission to the Holy Spirit propelled His Sonship to completeness.

Jesus walked in the pinnacle of Sonship in the earth. He lived in the realm of talking, acting and governing the elements of life from the Kingdom perspective. All things were under His subjection. He never spoke or acted like a servant or bastard child, afraid to take charge of His Father's affairs. Jesus pushed through the critics', religious fanatics and powers that resisted Him with a supernatural authority from the heavenly Father. He challenged and changed any misconception of His Father and His Kingdom held by the religious tyrants of His day. He ushered in a new order of God-like nature patterns for all humans to live in.

Chapter 12 End of Chapter Principles

∀ Jesus' name translated in the Greek is Jesus meaning 'Jehovah Saves' Saviour.

∀ 'Christ means Christos in Greek signifying 'Anointed King'.

∀ Jesus is the expressed image resemblance and character of the father.

∀ Jesus Christ is the essence of the Father; the first prototype of a Son.

∀ Jesus has all power and authority in heaven and in earth.

∀ Jesus' name has authority over every system, power, principality and being in the universe.

∀ Jesus came to give the Kingdom life.

Notes on Jesus' Position and Authority

Here are scriptural principles of Jesus as God with dominion, power and glory.

✎ The person of Jesus as the first of this new breed of sons. Jesus as the first Son begotten of the Father.

John 3:16 *"For God so love the world that He gave His only begotten Son, that whoever believeth in Him should not perish, but have everlasting life."* Jesus Christ's life and pattern of fellowship with God.

✎ The confirmation of the Father as seen with Jesus. Jesus was confirmed, accepted, validated and publicly owned by His Father.

! Jesus' mission is to raise Sons. **Jesus Assignment:-Hebrews 2:9** *"But we see Jesus, who was made a little lower than the* *angels for the suffering of death, crowned with glory and honour that he by the grace of God should taste death for every man."* **(vs. 10)** *"For it became Him, for whom are all things, and by whom are all things in bringing man sons unto glory, to make the captain of their salvation perfect through sufferings."*

Jesus came to reveal the Father in : **John 17:21** *"That's they may be one; as thou, Father, art in me, and I in thee that they also may be one in us that the world may believe that thou hast sent me."* **(vs. 22)** *"And the glory which thou gavest me I have given them; that they may be one, even as we are one."* Jesus is the High Priest, Bishop and Chief Apostle of His Sons.

🖉 The Name of Jesus has power. **Hebrews 2:11** *"For both He that sanctifieth and they who are sanctified are all of one: for which cause He is not ashamed to call them brethren."* **(vs. 12)** *"Saying, I will declare thy name unto my brethren, in the midst of the church will I sing praise unto thee."* **(vs. 13)** *"And again, I will put my trust in Him. And again, behold I and the children which God hath given me."* **(vs. 17)** *"Wherefore in all things it behoved him to be made like unto his brethren, that he might be a merciful and faithful high priest in things pertaining to God, to make reconciliation for the sins of the people."*

Chapter 13

The Nature of Man

!"

Scientific evidence and new philosophies understand that mankind is more than just a physical being, but is a complex being spiritually and emotionally. The links between the body and mind are more the ever before being intently studied. The question is examined into what makes man alive even when there remains a body and brain intact. Questions arise like what makes man different from an animal in reasoning abilities and behaviour. How it is that man can design, communicate, build and resolve complex issues? Lastly, what is the invisible part of the man where memories, thoughts, ideas and visions are stored?

The skeptics of the Bible are leaning closer towards the Genesis account of the creation of man in understanding humanity. Is man a Spirit or does he possess a spirit? This question is vital in the success of the believer. It clarifies man's position, authority and dominion endowed by God on him.

In fact, if man is to effectively release and unleash the greatness entrapped in his inner being then he must understand that he is more a spirit than a physical being. Medical doctors are now concluding in many instances that man possesses a body, a soul (mind) and have a spirit.

The word of God in the book of Genesis clearly outlines that from the beginning man's essence came from the Bible prints of the Creator's insights. It also gives in-depth detailed description of a creator, carefully and strategically moulding the universe. The skies and seas were arranged with indigenous creatures for the habitat and specific environment. We are suddenly shifted from the crawling, flying, swim-ming creatures to the one creature God takes special time to construct.

Genesis 2:7 states, *"And the LORD God formed man of the dust of the ground, and breathed into his nostrils the breath of life and man became a living soul."*

Genesis 2:21, *"And the LORD God caused a deep sleep to fall upon Adam and he slept: and He took one of his ribs, and closed up the flesh* *instead thereof;* **(vs. 22)***And the rib, which the LORD God had taken from man, made a woman, and brought her unto the man."*

The critics of the past are now becoming believers that man has always been a triune being. Even the masses of the scientific and medical researches are studying man holistically. In fact, the word of God stated from the very beginning that this is the essence of man. Conclusively, man by himself would be void and empty without life given breathe of God that entered his body at birth. The Old Testament gives the account of the creation, origins and beginnings of man. ('Man' being generic, including male and female). The animals, plants and other elements were spoken into being but man was constructed by the creator.

- **Genesis 1:3** *"And God said, let there be Light."*

- **Genesis 1:6** *"And God said, let there be a firmament in the midst of the waters, and let it divide the waters from the waters."*

- **(vs. 11)** *"And God said, let the earth bring forth grass, the herb yielding seed, and the fruit tree, yielding fruit after his kind, whose seed is in itself, upon the earth: and it was so."*

- **(vs. 20)** *"And God said, let the waters bring forth abundantly the moving creatures that* *hath life, and fowl that may fly above the earth in the open firma-ment of heaven."*

- **(vs. 24)** *"And God said, let the earth bring forth the living creatures after his kind, cattle, and creeping thing and beast as the earth his kind: and it was so."*

John: 1:12 *"But as many as received Him to them gave He power to become the Son of God, even to them that believe on his names:"*

(vs. 13) *"Which were born, not of blood, nor of the will of the flesh, nor of the will of man, but of God."*

The flesh represents the physical dimension of human (man's nature), which is mortal because of sin. This includes an understanding of the world through the five main senses of touch, taste, smell, hearing, and seeing. This complete system is wired in trillions of nerves and endocrine systems, which are constantly stemming information.

This complex information is streamed into the brain, via the eyes (what is seen), the ear (what is heard) and touch (what is felt). The output is the mouth and the motion of the body, which generally communicates what the mind or spirit, is receiving to release.

- The portion of the human is comprised of a body (man), which Genesis recounts gathering the dust of the ground and delicately forming a body (clay).

- The body is subject to the effects of the environment (heat, sun, radiation and pollution) and is subject to death because it is frail and temporal.

The psalmist David recounts that life is very volatile in **Psalm 103:14** *"For He (God) knoweth our frame; He remembereth that we are dust."* **(vs. 15)** *"As for man, his days are as grass" as a flower of the field, so he flourished* **(vs. 16)** *"For the wind passeth over it, and it is gone; and the place thereof shall know it no more."*

> **Psalm 104:30** *"thou sendest forth thy spirit…"*

- The soul refers primarily to that portion which is immaterial and is the seat of the invisible element in human beings. It is that portion in which persons think (mind; conscience; imagination), feel and have life. **Psalm 119:73** *"Thy hands have made me and fashioned me…"***John 6:63** *"It is the Spirit that quickened; the flesh profiteth nothing: the words that I speak unto you, they are spirit and they are life."*

Subsequent to the fall of Adam, humanity was no longer in the perfect state of innocence as prior. Therefore, humanity did not have the same spiritual, God-like attributes and qual-ities of that original state.

Jesus the second Adam came to restore a spiritual like-ness to God. **Matthew 11:27** *"All things are delivered unto me my Father: and no man knoweth the son, but the Father; neither knoweth any man the Father, save the Son and to whomsoever the Son will reveal him."*

The spirit "breath- Pneuma" is that inner invisible part of a human which gives them their identity. This is the part in which they think, mind, conscience, imagination, and feel.

The entire earth is filled with broken individuals who have lost insight into who they are, which is their identity. The greatest power is revealed when an individual understands what lies on the inside of them; more importantly an anointing is released when a believer understands their relationship and authority in God. God is the father and creator all things, and He has made provisions for you and I to possess those promises.

Matthew 6:8 *"Be not ye therefore like unto them: for your Father knoweth what things ye have need of therefore ye ask Him."*

Whereas the everlasting power and divinity of God are manifest in creation "Fatherhood in spiritual relationship through faith is the subject of New Testament revelation," and waited for the presence on earth of the son. The spiritual relationship is not universal.

'Bara' appears in a *Strong's Dictionary*. **Genesis 1:1** *"In the beginning God created the heavens and the earth."* The word created derives from a Hebrew Word 'Bara' (1254), which has the meaning, in a general sense of forming, making or producing. The word emphasizes the initiation of the object, not manipulating it or alters original creation. "The word possesses the understanding of bringing into existence." There is every reason to believe that 'Bara' was creation (exnihils) – out of nothing.

In contrast in **Genesis 1:26**, *"And God said, Let us make man in our image, after our likeness: and let them have dominion over the cattle, and over all the earth, and over every creeping thing that creepeth upon the earth."* 'Bara' portray's the thought of creation exnihils (out of nothing), which 'Asah' is broader in scope and dealt with refinement. In other words, the emphasis was fashioning the created objects.

The word 'Man' is noted two Hebrew Words – Adamah This Hebrew word is translated as 'earth', 'ground,' 'land' and 'country'. It is humus or arable land. Adamah supports water and plants.

The body of the first man, Adam, was formed form Adamah **(Genesis 2:7-9)** *"And the Lord God formed man of the dust of the ground, and breathe into his nostrils the breath of life, and man became a living soul."*

The term 'Image' is 'Tselem'. This noun signifies "likeness, resemblance, a representative figure or to shade. God made man in such a way as to reflect some of His own perfections – perfect in knowledge, righteousness and holi-ness, with dominion over the creatures. *Tselem i*s not an exact replica. It is only a show of a thing, representing the original in an imprint manner, lacking the essential characteristics (reality) of the original. Even though man has been tarnished by sin as a result of the fall, he still maintains the essential nature of God being.

1.) **The word** 'likeness' -this noun means resemblance, simulator, image, model, pattern, and shade.

The word dust comes from the Hebrew 'Aphar'- means dust, fine particles of earth, dry earth, and fine dust. It also means soil, loam, and clay. The usual meaning is dust or loose earth.

The word 'breath' – It means a puff of air, a breath, breathing, panting. The Hebrew word Neshamah means the Spirit of God implanting life, wisdom, and divine inspiration.

The word 'ruach' means anything which passes quickly, the air put in motion by divine breathe; the blast of God. **Ruach** can be used of the divine miraculous power by which inanimate things begin to move, the spirit of God, Holy Spirit.

The word 'chayah' means to live, exist, enjoy life, to live anew, to make alive, quicken. **'Chayeh'** has it's meaning is: living, alive, has life, remain alive, and sustain life. God is the source of life. **Psalms 36:9, 139:13, 1.** *"For with thee is the fountain of life in the light shall we see light."*

The word 'soul' 'Nephesh' arises from 'naphash'. It is the soul by which the body lives or example continues to live by drawing breath.

The Hebrew concept of man was the inner self and the outer appearance. That example is what is to oneself and what one appears to those who observe him. However, the source of the nephesh of animals is the ground, but God is the source of the nephesh of Adam. The term is translated as "Heart" connotation the inner man sometimes it is referred to:

The word in the Hebrew (*Lexical Aids* to the Old Testament) that paints a clearer picture, 'apar' (6083) – This noun represents the porous loose earth on the ground, or "dust". In its first biblical occurrence, "apar appears to mean this porous loose earth: It can also signify "dry crumble mortar or plaster."

The body is what I would consider the least of the enti-ties that make up man. Reason in consideration is the fact that man's body is controlled and does what either his Spirit states or what h are mind desires. Hence the body (material) is subjected to the immaterial or invisible. However what is invisible (for example your thoughts) may not be seen but is manifested in the body.

Mankind: Image -God made us in some resemblance likeness, illusion or shade of His person. You and I whether we choose to accept or reject it, reflect some of God's perfection – perfect in knowledge, righteousness and holiness, with dominion over the creatures. We have been empowered with the material of reasoning, creativity, and vision and goal orientation and able to speak things into happening. God also gave us from the understanding of the Hebrews 'Tselem' and immaterial portion called a soul. Likeness (1823) – Dhemuth: It means **likeness, resemblance, simili-tude, image, model, pattern, and shape.** Both of these words constitute a mental picture of man, sadly tarnished by the snares of sin or sanctified have been designed by God. This is why we observe even in unsaved person with the creative and intellectual powers to form huge corporations, engage space explorations, endeavor scientific phenomena (cloning, test-tube babies) and construction of large build-ings. If we were to examine God's creation of the universe it was through His spoken word. God gave us a strong will and a powerful force of faith that pushes us to accomplishing all our desires. Most notable our Father is a Spirit; therefore we too are spiritual creatures.

However, because God is omnipotent, humanity is no way on the same level with the Creator. Hence, if we are to fulfill what God has trapped on the inside of our brains we need to maintain a relationship with the Creator. The Father is our mirror; the longer we stay away from looking at Him the sooner we forget who we are in Christ. The longer we look at our Creator, the more conscious we become of the unwanted blemished and scars of sin that ruin our image. It is when we see our Creator we cry out for repentance.

We must obey the will of the Father; for it is not only the church's order. It is the order of the Son, and God is concern with man's communion and fellowship rather than oppressive rituals. We are sons, heirs of God and joint heirs with Christ. He is not ashamed to call us brothers, all that the Father has been declared to us is our possession. *"The earth is the Lord's and the fullness thereof."*

James 1:17 *"Every good and perfect gift is from above, coming down from the <u>Father of heavenly lights,</u> who does not change like shifting shadows."* **James 1:18** *"He chose to give us birth through the word of truth, that we might be kind of first fruits of all he created."*

<u>The Father of Spirits and Souls</u>:-

Hebrews 12:9 *"Moreover, we have all had Fathers who disciplined us and we respected them for it. How much more should we submit to the Father of our Spirits and live!"*

The term 'Av'; or Father means the begetter, parent; progenitor, forefather, ancestor, an originator creator, inventor. It also means a benefactor or guardian; a head, chief ruler, a Lord, master, teacher; an advisor, counsellor, one in authority. The 'Messiah' is called the Everlasting Father).

Isaiah 9:6 *"For unto us a child is born, unto us a son is given: and the government shall be upon His shoulder and His name shall be called wonderful, counsellor, the mighty God, the <u>Everlasting Father</u>, the prince of peace."*

God (Jehovah) is the Father of Israel, **Isaiah 63:16** *"But you are our <u>Father</u> though Abraham does not know us or Israel acknowledge us; you, O Lord, are our Father redeemer from of old is your name."*

Jeremiah 31:9 *"They will come with weeping they will pray as I bring them back. I will lead them beside streams of water on a level path where they will not stumble, because I am Israel's father and Ephraim is my firstborn son."*

Malachi 2:10 tell us that God is the Father of all people. He is especially the "<u>protector</u>" or "father of the fatherless'. "A father of the fatherless and a judge of the widows is God in His Holy habitation."

Jehovah God is the Father of all creations and sustainer of all that exist. His nature as Father is seen with his intimacy with man-Adam. God's nature intended in His wonderful plan to continue his kind or his 'gene'. In the nature course of marriage, couple decides to produce a product of their love, an offspring after themselves. This offspring has the same genes or genetic makeup of the parents. **Ephesians 4:6** *"One God and Father of all, who is above all, and in you all."*

The key to developing any relationship is communica-tion. This involves the parties involved sharing and talking on a constant basis. The Father requires the same open line of dialogue with Him. There is occasional difficulty because we can talk to God in prayer. We can spend quiet time in His presence or whisper a call for direction about matters.

The key theme for this possession is obedience to the Spirit of our Father. To them that are led by the Spirit are the <u>Sons of God</u>. This led is a total surrender. It reminds me of childhood, where an innocent, obedient child trusting follows the direction of their father in the mall. They are fully assured that their daddy will not lead him astray.

That child never goes out in front of the father or too far. However, they stay close to the body of the father. This is the attachment the Father desires for us, the close walk with him. He does not want us to run out to far ahead without feeling His presence nearby. We are not to lag behind and allow His presence to go without us thereby being left stranded and isolated in a world; lost and confused.

The word 'led' also suggest an acceptance to wanting to be directed carefully and strategically through life.

John 17:25 *"O righteous Father, the world had not known thee: but I have known* *thee, and these have known that thou have sent me."*

God's intention for the creation was relationship and not a dictatorship for humanity. There is a strong covenant involved in the family. Intimacy is natural and identity is formed. In the natural family, a bond is created between the members. This bond is emotional, in which the individual have the opportunity to express their feelings of anger, disappointment and joy in a loving environment. God is so different; His desire is to be an active father in our lives.

He desires to reward our obedience and to rebuke our errors to bring us to our destiny. There is a blessing stored for obedience to the voice of the Father. Persons not of the lineage of Abraham were outside of the covenant of the Fatherhood blessings. We were outcast to inheritance. We were destined to fail and cut off from the promises God had for his children. In the book of Exodus the Patriarch

Abraham was proclaimed to be the Father of a new breed of people. Everything was sealed by God to be received by the descendants of Abraham.

Adam was the first natural father of all mankind. He was the perfect idea of God, but due to his fall; God began the process of rising up a seed or generation of faith people through Abraham. Abraham became the "Father of Faith" or the Father of Promise. Jesus completed the work of Fatherhood through faith by raising son by the Spirit of God. Who were not once a people but became the people of God.

Jesus made it possible to engraft all races, creeds and people into a promise that was not there own. A new family was established through faith.

All the deeds were transferred, there was a transfer of Sonship and a new identity was formed for the Family of God through Jesus Christ. We have become adopted as Sons of God through Jesus Christ. We have become adopted as Sons into the family of God covenant.

II Corinthians 6:18 *"And will be a Father unto you, and ye shall be my sons and daughters, said the Lord Almighty."*

John 8:42 *"Jesus said unto them, if God were your Father, ye would love me: for I proceeded forth and came from God; neither came I of myself, but He sent me."*

Romans 8:17 *"And if children, then heirs; heirs of God and joint heirs with Christ; if so be that we suffer with him, that we may be also glorified together."*

You can then step outside of your earthy heritage and become a part of the royal family of God. As such you become a joint heir with Jesus. **(Romans 8:17**) and are made in the righteousness of God. **(Romans 5:17)** In essence, all of the promises of God become yours.

> **Mathew 5:45** *"That ye may be children of your Father which is in Heaven: for He maketh His son to rise on the evil and on the good, and sendeth rain on the just and the unjust."*

"Be ye therefore perfect, even as your Father which is in Heaven is perfect." Hence this shows that man is partially make in the image and likeness of God and the Bible records in **John 4:24** that God is a spirit and they that worship Him must worship Him in spirit and in truth. Man is limited in wisdom, insights and the accomplishment in certain things by himself. It takes the presence of God in our lives and mortal bodies that push us beyond what we could have naturally accomplish. With the Holy Spirit, we can become limitless. Hallelujah to our God and Father Jesus Christ!!!!

Chapter 13 End of Chapter Principles:

∀ Man has a body, soul and spirit.

∀ Mankind through Adam was created in the image, likeness and nature of the heavenly Father.

∀ Mankind's body was created by the dust of the earth.

∀ Jehovah, our Father is the creator of everything.

∀ Those led by the spirit are the Sons of God.

∀ We are engrafted into a great inheritance of Abraham through Jesus Christ.

Chapter 14

Understanding Sons & Sonship

!"

Romans 8:14 "For as many as are led the Son of God."

"The Kingdom of God doesn't come with outward appearance. It manifests itself through the life of Christ that is manifested in His people." (Sons and Sonship- Hancliff)

Luke 17:21 "Neither shall they say, Lo here! Or lo there! For, behold, the kingdom of God is within you."

The Spirit of Christ is a person of government and authority. The Father is calling out administrators and governors for His Kingdom. He is calling out people who can take the responsibility of establishing His Kingdom; ruling and reigning with Him. Sonship allows for building the Kingdom of God through their lives. We have been called of God to Sonship to service and partnership with the Father.

The word *'teknon'* from the Greek translates "one born" and denotes immaturity. It is never used of Christ when He is spoken of as the Son of God. **Romans 8:16** *"The Spirit itself beareth witness with our Spirit, that we are the children of God."*

There is a different Greek word used above for 'sons.' The Greek word is 'Huios' and translated into English, it means descendant or offspring. It denotes maturity or one full grown.

The word is translated from the Greek word "huiothesia" and it means "the placing of a son," the placing of one who has walked in the relationship of childhood into a position of responsibility as a mature son. **Galatians 4:5** *"That we might receive the adoption of sons."*

It is God's mind to bring about the change that takes place when a child is recognized as an adult. A child, who takes the responsibilities of a Son, is able to take on the responsibility of kingdom building. Adoption speaks of position and not relationship.

God is aiming for a relationship of gradual responsi-bilities. He wants us to be workers together with Him, to take on a full partnership in the business of His kingdom government.

Individuals become Sons of God by believing and by submission to the Holy Spirit. All that is required is belief in the sincere mandate of the Father. We become Sons by obedience to the Spirit.

God has a purpose for son

The Father will use obedient sons to fulfill His purpose in the earth. He will establish the Kingdom in the earth through the strategic, networking ministry of those who have entered into matured Sonship. He will use the sons to deliver the whole creation from the bondage of corruption.

Jesus had such an intimacy with God the Father. It was one of complete submission agreement and communions he demonstrated to us. The power of agreement is very strong; "How can the two walk unless they agree?" Jesus was committed to conducting the affairs of His father.

His daily life was surrounded and consumed the Father's will and purpose. He was sensitive to represent the Father's interests at all times. He learnt obedience through sufferings. Jesus' main objective was to promote and establish the Kingdom of God. He wanted God's rule of government and praises on the earth. Jesus spent quality time in the presence of God to hear the direction and instruction from Him. He also went into His presence to receive strength. In God's presence there is fullness of Joy.

The Father's plans for Sons

What are the affairs of the Father? Firstly, the Father designed a specific role and assignment for each individual to fulfill. Another human can recognize giftedness or talent blossoming. However, only quality time asking the Father and fellowshipping with Him will true purpose be discov-ered. Consider any relationship, one would recognize that only with spending quality time together would be the dreams of those persons and their emotions are understood. Most importantly, both parties involved begin to learn the very essence and character of the other individual. In many wonderful moments even ones own character is discovered. One would discover personal weakness and strengths and would have to make various changes in one's own character to relate in the relationship involved.

This analogy is exactly how our Father longs for a loving relationship with his children. Daddy wants us to tell Him when we hurt and what makes us upset. He wants for us to share our vision and goals with Him. He wants to fulfill them for us. He desires to mentor and developed our lives into the beautiful thought out plans He has for our lives. Papa wants to share our most intimate moments of broken secrets; things in our lives that no one else knows. He wants to heal those shameful events of our hidden past. Father wants to heal our guilty, unbearable, shameful past. He longs to gently settle our shaky minds and revive our identity in Him.

The Father desires to share His <u>dreams, passions and emotions</u> with His Sons. Similar to any loving father, daddy wants to express what grieves Him. He excitedly waits to tell and show His children the precious gifts He has waiting. How about sitting as He speaks His plans for His family? Lastly, He wants to safely cradle us in His arm and delicately pour His assurance that we His Sons and His prized possession.

The Father yearns for the restoration of His Sons. This word son from the original language and text has two words. One word is 'Tekna', which connotes a young child, in reference to scripture; it suggests that all of humanity is the offspring or creation of God. However, the second term of 'Huios' refers to a mature son.

The Father perfects Sons

Jehovah God is the Father of all creation and sustainer of all that exists. His nature as Father is seen with His intimacy with man-Adam. The body of Christ is at a time of great movement of the Spirit. God is pouring out new insights and revelation about His word as He equips and prefect the church, His bride, to meet Him.

One of the last battles of the Spirit will be to perfect the Christian believer. This word 'perfect' does mean that every believer will be whole or complete in all areas of their lives. This maturing process has been the heart of the Father God for many generations as He slowly revealed His nature to mankind throughout history. This is observed especially with the Hebrew people and now the church of Jesus Christ.

God is bound by His word and covenant to reestablish His relationship with mankind after Adam fell in the Garden of Eden. He is concerned with fellowship with His prized creation humans. God is seeking to restore the relationship of Father-ship to mankind. Adam had an intimate relationship with the Father among great levels of relation of God and man, creator and creative being. It was a Father-Son relationship.

God as a father had a heart like any earthly father to bear an offspring, a seed that would continue His affairs. Similarly, as earthly fathers desire a seed that resembles them and would continue the name and the genetics or the seed of the father. Hence God desire to conform man truly after His image and likeness. These words suggest a number of qualities and characteristics of God and hence man. "God is a Spirit and they that worship Him must worship Him in spirit and in truth."

Hebrews 12:5 *"And you have forgotten that of encouragement that addresses you as sons: My son, do not make light of the Lord's discipline and do not lose heart when He rebukes you,"*

(vs. 6) *"Because the Lord disciplines those He loves, and punishes everyone He accepts as a Son."*

Hence, mankind is the very genetic seed of God. Man is the gene of God, unlike the other creatures that were made by the very thought of God. God proposed to make man with His very hand to breathe or place His very nature into man ('Pneuma' – 'breathe of Spirit').

Adam had a relationship with God among levels of relations of God and man, creator and creative being. He had a Father – Son relationship. On the other hand, one of the messiah's enthronement names is "Eternal Father" *"And His name shall be called Wonderful, Counsellor, The mighty God, the Everlasting Father, and the Prince of Peace."*
(Isaiah 9:6)

Many today are in search of true identity. This is one of the greater problems in our world. This world is filled with people who lack an understanding of who they are. Many are searching aimlessly in all areas, including education, career, finances and relationships to occupy the void in their lives. The true identity of the born again Christian believer comes from knowing where they come from or in other terms that their Father is. Understanding who we are is pivotal in fore-seeing where we are going. Who we are tells us our strengths in various areas of our lives and also our weakness. It gauges our self -confidence and measures our potential. It deter-mines our comfort in developing meaningful relationships with others.

Fatherhood is a strong form of self-regulation for developing a person's character development. Naturally, a father in the home provides a young girl with security, self – perception and a model of good men in her life. Likewise, a young man forms his early perception of maleness and identity of manhood from his father.

The whole family is centered on the order of father. Similarly, in the spiritual realm, our heavenly Father wants to import destiny, direction and daily development into the lives of His children. This special interest in His creation is not always received by many but is acquired through Sonship. This is a covenant relationship inherited through Jesus Christ and sealed by God's Spirit verifying that we are His children.

Romans 8:14 *"For as many as are by the Spirit of God, they are the sons of God."*

(vs. 15) *"The Spirit itself beareth witness with our spirit, that we are the children of God."*

Jesus, the first Son became the one through whom came many Sons of the Father. Through sonship we learn the inheritance God has delegated to His sons. We understand the Royal family line that runs through our veins. We are a part of a kingly family; the children of a King.

Romans 8:9 *"But ye are not in the flesh, but in the Spirit if so be that the Spirit of God dwells in you. Now if any man has not the Spirit of Christ, he is none of His."***(vs. 14)** *"For as many as are led by the Spirit of God, they are the sons of God.* **(vs. 15)** *"For ye have not received the Spirit of bondage again to fear; but ye have received the Spirit of adoption, whereby we cry Abba Father."***(vs. 16)** *"The Spirit itself beareth witness with our spirit, that we are the children of God :(* **vs. 17)** *"And if children, them heirs; heirs of God and joint – heirs with Christ." If so be that we suffer with Him, that we may be also glorified together."*

Paul the writer of Romans, explosively reveals the power of the believer in Jesus Christ. Paul summarizes the nature of every human's potential to become a son of God. He expresses the life of the spirit. Spiritual sonship is the life led by the 'paraceletos', the Holy Spirit. Sonship is a life submitted to the direction of the Holy Spirit. The heavenly Father yearned to establish His continuous stream of fellow-ship and love when He created His son Adam in the book of Genesis. Adam was to represent the expressed nature, character and authority of the Heavenly Father on earth as the Father ruled in Heaven.

Adam was to propagate the spiritual righteous DNA of the Father throughout the ages: - human offspring. Mankind was to rule the gardens, the animals and the earth realm and be co-heir the spiritual realm with the Father. Adam was to expand the kingdom rulership of the Father in the earth with complete obedience and harmony with daddy.

All of Adam's offspring was to rule in harmony and righteous order and alignment with the natural commands of the Father. Adam represented the spiritual sons of God and the gene was to continue in power; protected from the destructive elements of sin and the environment.

The book of beginnings, Genesis, expresses the disconnected relationship of Adam, the son with the Father. Adam dishonoured the relationship with the Father and lost the benefits of being a Son of a King. Adam lost fellowship through the Holy Spirit's presence that gave him supernatural power, wisdom, creativity, council and streams of God-like abilities. Most importantly, Adam's 'God – like' genes were mutated and now He operated in a lower level of function. It made it impossible to continue the seed or DNA of God in purity to humanity throughout the generations. Adam lost abilities to govern the affairs of the earth in order to the Father's heart. He was disconnected with the purposes of the Father's mind, and the vision of the Father through Adam was clouded.

The glorious agenda of Kingdom conquest and partnership ruler-ship with man in the earth seemed threatened and impossible. The enemies of the Kingdom agenda of the Heavenly Father mocked and chuckled to the demise of the Father's dream. It seemed as if the Father's business was about to hit bankruptcy. He was going to lose all of His shares over the earth. The son had rebelliously given the power of attorney to a corrupt fired employee, the devil. Satan, the devil was now the major share holder over the earth by technicality and severed man from his creator.

Through manipulation in the Garden, Satan legally acquired the power of attorney and ownership over the earth. He also got lease to every human that would be produced by Adam. All men therefore were born is sin and shaped in iniquity; and the seed or DNA of Satan was injected into the genetic architect of man. Satan had clones to expand his diabolical seed to the earth through the sons of God.

For thousands of years the Kingdom of God suffered violent attacks. The restoration of a race that would revive the genetics of the Father suffered tremendous distortion. The scriptures account the patriarch Abraham, as being the forerunner of God's agenda to reclaim the seed and re-establish His sons in the earth.

The spiritual climate was overcast with wickedness in the earth for hundreds of years. Immorality, disorder and rebellion to the commands of the Father were prevalent.

Humanity had drifted furlongs away from the original vision of the father's empire. Man now dimly mirrored the nature, character, love and righteous rulership of their heavenly Father. The Father was so disgusted that He grieved and was sorrowful that He ever created man. Mankind became outside children, bastards who had no God-like identity. In fact, they had taken a new identity and resembled the rebellious, distorted, corrupted, adopted step-father Satan. Mankind, from the fall of Adam now worked in the family business of Satan, as co-heirs and executive directors in the Kingdom of Darkness.

The scriptures give vivid accounts of the heavenly Father's passive and patient plead for humanities fellowship. Yet through His plea and tremendous promises, mankind through the children of Abraham rejected Him. He continuously forgave and protected the children of Israel during their progression in life.

The Father had found a people to begin the restorative process of re-establishing sons in the earth. His awesome presence in man was banded from communication with him. His holy presence was key to the 'Zoë' life of His sons. The 'Zoe' life is the 'God-life' that was in the order and righteousness of the Father. 'Zoe' life was the life of the Holy Spirit in which the identity of being a Son of God was important on the minds of every son. The 'Zoe' life in the Holy Spirit was the existence where the laws of the Father were imbedded in the minds of the Sons.

The Parakletos, the comforter, and advisor would intimately direct the sons into truth and righteousness. 'Paracletos', the Holy Spirit would unleash in every obedient son rivers of insights wisdom, revelation of the father's nature.

The Holy Spirit in the sons would empower them to walk in great authority on behalf of the Father over every situation and circumstance. The Spirit filled son would be protected from disease and death and hence walk daily in the 'Shalom' of the Father.

Sons would experience the 'shalom', meaning the **'completeness, wholeness and prosperity'** in every area of their lives. This was the Father's delight to celebrate in the wealth and shalom of His sons.

The descendants of Abraham were eyed by the Father to restore His plan of Co-ownership with mankind in the earth.

However, there was a barrier to the fulfillment of maturation of children of Sons through the Parakletos. The nations lacked the indwelling and resting upon by the presence of the Holy Spirit. Mankind was repulsive to the saturation of the Father's Holy presence and the training of man was delayed. The Father had a brilliant plan to conquer this minor dilemma. He established the King's tutoring services. This service was to govern and prepare the children underage spiritually to matured sons. This was until the moment when access would be granted in the earth for the indwelling tutor of the Holy Spirit. The Holy Spirit would then continue and complete the maturation of the spirit and mind of the sons to the heart vision and purpose of the Father. The Holy Spirit would empower the sons to overcome and destroy the contaminated gene of Satan in their flesh nature. He would train the lost sons on how to whip the desires of self and sin and bring them subject to the laws and order of the Father Holy nature.

Paracletos, the Holy Spirit would equip and activate the sons, in their own unique way to build relentlessly the Kingdom of the Father in the earth. The sons would be consumed with the reclaiming of all spheres for the Father's sovereign rulership.

Galatians 4:1-9

(vs. 1) *"Now I say, that the heir as long as he is a child, differeth nothing from a servant though he be lord of all;*

(vs. 2) *"But is under tutors and governors until the time appointed of the father.*

(vs. 3) *"Even so we, when we were children; were in bondage under the elements of the world:*

(vs. 4) *"But when the fullness of the time was come, God sent forth His Son, made of a woman, made under the law,*

(vs. 5) *"To redeem them that was under the law, that we might receive the adoption of sons.*

(vs. 6) *"And because ye are sons, God hath sent forth the Spirit of his son unto your hearts, crying, Abba, Father.*

(vs. 7) *"Wherefore thou art no more a servant but a son; and if a son; then an heir to God through Christ."*

(vs. 8) *"Howbeit then, when ye knew not God, ye did service unto them which by nature are no gods.*

(vs. 9) *But now, after that ye have known God, or rather are known of God, how turn ye again to the weak and beggarly elements, whereunto ye desire again to be in bondage?*

Paul in the book of Galatians magnificently summarizes the order and restoration of the sons of God. Built with every person is the potential to become a son of God and heir to the kingdom of the Heavenly Father. All humanity outside of the obedience and adoption of the heavenly father is an heir identity. Hence an heir outside of the relationship and knowledge of their inheritance is no greater than a servant.

For example a child of an owner of a food franchise chain. That child has access to all of his father's business, resources and influences. However, the father in an effort to mature the son hires him as a janitor in one of the restaurants. The son enjoys the experience and salary he makes but is ordered by his supervisors daily to do manual task. That son is learning responsibility and experiencing maturity as he climbs that ladder of success to now become a cashier. Sadly, his father dies and leaves the entire franchise with over one hundred stores to the son. However, disturbingly the son is unaware that he has been left the franchise in a will and continues to work as a cashier.

This son is ignorant of his true identity as the father's heir to all his assets. He is blinded to his new position of authority and ownership. In parallel, many persons live in the same disposition with the heavenly father in the earth.

Millions of humans have the inheritance of the earth and the indwelling presence of the Holy Spirit's resource. But they are unaware of it. Many prefer to work tiredly as a servant and not take authority as the delegated owners of all the heavenly Father has for them in the earth.

Humanity struggles with the identity as being lords of all but instead settles for being servants. Similarly, scenarios throughout scripture are in current times. Humanity has been in the restricted halls of the University of Life. Religion and religious activity now forms the world's philosophy and cage the lost Sons of God operation. Rituals and spiritual activities institutionalize the bastard sons until they receive the liberty that is in Jesus Christ.

It is through the only begotten Son Jesus Christ, that access is granted directly to fellowship with the Father's portfolio. Jesus came to mend the gap between the father and the wayward sons of the earth. Jesus came to restore the kingdom life in the mentality of the sons. Thoroughly, Jesus took His own blood and DNA and shed it so that mankind can have access to the Father's restored nature.

Jesus came to restore the lineage of spiritual sons and daughters in the earth. He became the perfect prototype of the Father's nature, love, essence, character, authority and order in the earth once again. Mankind now had a model of the Father's express image in the earth. Jesus came to call many sons back to the Father. The lease of Satan's reign over the earth and strangle hold on the image of God's fallen son is over.

The key that held the sons in bondage and shackle was taken by the Son Jesus. He transacted an act of sacrifice of His life. He through legal rights and humanly partnership crafted a plan and executed restoration of fellowship of man and the Father through the Holy Spirit.

Jesus reintroduces the kingdom of the Father is was recruiting volunteers of sons into partnership for conquest in the earth. He demonstrated His power over disease, the environment, nature and sin. Jesus spoke harshly to disease and told them to leaves the bodies of 'lost sons'. He rebuked the wind and waves. He walked on water; told a fig tree to dry up and it did.

He walked victoriously reprogrammed the DNA of sin implanted in man through rebellion in the Garden of Eden. Jesus triumphed over the nature of Satan and violently resisted any nature to partner with Satan to establish the devil's Kingdom.

He overcame and dispelled demons out of operating in the realm of this earth. Jesus' accounts clearly indicated that He was about re-establishing the business of the kingdom in the earth. His Father's business was about to be revived out of collapse. A new manager and CEO was in town and plans of restoration of the Father affairs were imminent. He requested the Father to restore Him to His former state of glorious power; authority, and wealth after His death on the cross.

Previously Jesus requested from the owner that the advisor who was with Him always be given to the new sons that He has chosen for the kingdom cooperation. The Parakletos would stay with them, upon them and even in them, forever to accelerate the maturation process. The advisor is the person of the Holy Spirit would continue to remind the sons of the nature and purpose of Jesus lead them to all that is truthfully and convict them of rebellion to the nature of the Father.

The Holy Spirit would also by legal transfer adopt new sons and process them into true sons who would walk in great inheritance.

Galatians 4:5 *"To redeem them that were under the law, that we might receive the* *adoption of sons.* **(vs. 6)** *"Because ye are sons, God hath sent forth the Spirit of His Son into your hearts, crying, Abba Father.*

(vs. 7) *"Wherefore thou art no more a servant, but a son; and if a son, then an heir of God through Christ."*

Spiritual sonship is not a concept limited to sex or gender but of identity in the heavenly Father through Jesus Christ. For the scriptural text sons represent male and female, boy and girl, young and old, including all nationalities that accept Jesus Christ as the Saviour.

Spiritual sonship represents the disposition of mankind to the submission, obedience and direction of the Holy Spirit's voice. Sons are the matured believer who has grown from the lifestyle of sin and who walks in the nature, image and power of Jesus.

Spiritual sonship produces power to **reign** and to **exer-cise** authority. The Bible says, *"But as many as received Him, to them gave He power to become the sons of God."*

Power is the ability to get results. Therefore, the mark indicating whether or not one walks in spiritual sonship is one's ability to get positive results. Achieving your place of spiritual sonship means: "Spiritual sons are defined as men and women who by the power of God brings deliverance and liberty to mankind. Spiritual sons disarm forces of wickedness and bring the creature out of the bondage of corruption into the glorious liberty of the son of God. Spiritual sons are those who through an understanding of their divine nature act like God on the earth. Sons are those who understand their divine nature." (Apostle Emmanuella Mchatton- "The Turning Point").

Romans 8:19 *"For the whole creation (all nature) waits expectantly and longs earnestly for God's – not God's son, but for God's sons to be made known (waits for the revealing, the disclosing g of their sonship."*

To be a son of God means that you recognize the nature of God residing within you. That realization will move you above the natural, through the power of the Holy Spirit, to the realm of the supernatural.

The seed potential of sonship is on the inside of every person who's born into this earth.

Galatians 4:1-2 says: *"Now I say, that the heir, as long as he is a child, differeth nothing from a servant, though he be lord of all; "But is under tutors and governors until the time appointed of the Father."*

Authentic spiritual sonship requires righteousness, earnest prayer, integrity and knowing the authority of Jesus' name. Jesus' name releases the anointing the electric current that flows and gives power in the lives of His children.

Sonship Scriptures:

I John 3:9 *"No one who is born of God Will continue to sin, because God's seed remain in him; he cannot go on sinning, because he has been born of God. This is how we know who the children of God are and who the children of the devil are; anyone who does not do what is right is not a child of God; nor is anyone who does not love His brother."*

Romans 8:14 *"For as many as are led by the Spirit of God, they are the sons of God."*

(vs. 15) *"For ye have not received the spirit of bondage again to fear; but ye have received the Spirit of adoption, whereby we cry Abba Father."*

(vs. 16) *"The Spirit itself beareth witness with our spirit that we're the children of God."*

The Father's plan as defined by the book of Genesis was to establish His kingdom into the earth realm. He in His infi-nite wisdom crafted the earth and heavens.

He strategically planted a wonderful garden for His precious son, Adam. He formed man in His own image and likeness to express His **character, nature, love and <u>kingly</u> authority in the earth.**

The nature of the Father was vividly express as God, source, protection, and King. Each of His characteristic features portrays a nature the mankind can unlock and operate in while living in the earth. Each individual possess the capacity built into their spiritual gene to reproduce the nature of the Father in the earth.

The heavenly Father as God has a desire like any earthly papa to produce offspring, or seed to continue the affairs of His kind. The Father desired a seed that resembles Him and would continue the name and genetics of the father. Hence from the book of Genesis the heavenly Father made mankind in the very genetics of God. Man is the DNA of God, unlike the other creatures that were made by the very thought of God. There is no mention that the colourful peacock, flamboyant flamingo or ferocious lion were made in the image and likeness of the Father.

Jehovah God is the progenitor and Father of all creation and sustainer of all that exists. His nature as Father has been expressed with His intimacy with man

– Adam and creation. Adam had a relationship with God among levels of relation of God. He demonstrated the protocol of a Father-Son relationship in His pre-fallen state.

In the book of beginnings, the Father is seen talking directly to Adam. The Father gave him all the resources need to be successful in the order and righteousness of the Father. The Father walked and fellowshipped with Adam in the cool of the day. The relationship was strongly intact.

The Father longs for complete fellowship with every human being. We have the tremendous opportunity to be reunited with our God, Father and friend, Hallelujah!!!

Chapter 14 End of Chapter Principles

∀ The Spirit of Christ is a person of government and authority.

∀ The Father is calling out administrators and governors for His Kingdom.

∀ He is calling out people who can take the responsibility of establishing His Kingdom; ruling and reigning with Him.

∀ The Father's plan as defined by the book of Genesis was to establish His kingdom into the earth realm

∀ Mankind is the very genetic seed of God. Man is the gene of God, unlike the other creatures that were made by the very thought of God.

∀ Jehovah God is the progenitor and Father of all creation and sustainer of all that exists. His nature as Father has been expressed with His intimacy with man – Adam and creation

∀ Authentic spiritual sonship requires righteousness, earnest prayer, integrity and knowing the authority of Jesus' name.

∀ Jesus reintroduces the kingdom of the Father is was recruiting volunteers of sons into partnership for conquest in the earth.

Chapter 15

The Genetics of a Son

!"

The scope of the DNA of man and the expression of the Father through mankind is the key to understanding Sonship. The sons of God represent the extension of the Father in the earth. Adam lost the initial manifestation of the Father's nature that was built into His genetic essence. The rebellious fall of Adam to Satan caused the severing of fellowship of God and mankind. It also isolated mankind from intimate relationship with His source. God the Father's fellowship would have sparked Adam to continue to know

His father.

The Father's desire was to propagate through Adam and his lineage, His nature. He wanted to continue His seed of a God-man in the earth. He wanted to continue a species unlike the angels in the heavens. The Father did not want to reproduce the elders or created beings as mention in the book of revelation but He wanted human sons.

The Father wanted sons who would have the heart and vision of the Father in expanding His Kingdom in the hearts of men. Sons resemble the Father both spiritually and His desires for sons particularly those who have submitted to the obedience of the Spirit of God.

Adam represents the nature, character, and wealth of the Father.

Sons of God received self-awareness from the Father. They express the identity of the Father. Sons were destined to conduct business on behalf of the Father in the earth.

Sons Scriptures:

I John 5:1 *"Whose believeth that Jesus is the Christ is born of God: and everyone that loveth Him that begat loveth Him also that is begotten of Him."*

(vs. 4) *"For whatsoever is born of God over cometh the world and this is the* victory that over-comes the world, even our faith."

(vs. 5) "Who is he that over cometh the world, but he that believeth that Jesus is the Son of God?"

I John 5:18 "We know that whosoever is born of God sinneth not, but he that is begotten of God keepeth himself and that wicked one toucheth him not."

(vs. 20) "And we know that the Son of God is come and hath given us an understanding that we may know Him that is true, and we are in Him that is true even in His son Jesus Christ. This is the true God, and eternal life."

II John 1:9 "Whosoever trangresseth and abideth not in the doctrine of Christ hath not God. He that abideth in the doctrine of Christ he hath both the Father and the son."

John 1:11-13 "He came unto his own and his own received him not."

(vs. 12) "But as many as received him, to them gave He power to become the sons *of God, even to them that believe on His name."*

(vs. 13) *"Which were born, not of blood, nor of the will neither of the flesh nor of the will of man but of God."*

John 17:22 *"And the glory which thou gavest me. I have given them; that they may be on even as we are one.*

(vs. 23) *"I in them and thou in me, that they may be made perfect in one; and that the world may know that thou hast sent me, and hast loved them as thou hast loved me."*

(vs. 25) *"O righteous Father, the world hath not known thee: but I have known thee, and these have known that thou least sent me."*

(vs. 26) *"And I have declared unto them thy name; and will declare it that the love wherewith thou hast loved me may be in them, and I in them."*

Sons Unveiled in the Earth

Romans 8:14 *"For as many as are led by the Spirit of God, they are the sons of God."*

Paul, the writer of the book of Romans presents the invitation to all humanity to reconnect with our source, the heavenly Father. Re-connected fellowship of man with the Father through Jesus' blood sacrifice allows the Holy Spirit to wire the hearts of man and God. The invitation was extended to the listeners and readers in ancient Roman but also transcends to contemporary times. The above scripture strongly contents that as many are **led by** the Spirit of God can become the Sons.

The concept led by (71) in the *Lexical Aids* to the New Testament is the Greek word **'Ago'** meaning **to lead, to lead along, to bring, to carry.** The clearest meaning is to lead gently and without violence by a director. The term 'led' by can also be expressed as to lead, rule, and govern. Hence, to as many persons who would allow the gentle, peaceful governing and rule of the Holy Spirit they have a privilege of being a son. A son must be fully surrendered to fulfillment; passively allow the Holy Spirit to navigate their lives through the meanders of life. They must allow the Spirit of God to channel the course of the compass and sail them into the destiny and purpose of the Father. The sons must be confident that every circumstance that is experienced on the path is being used by the captain, the Holy Spirit, to mature us.

These apparent barriers of life in the like of a son who is obedient to the skillful leading of the Holy Spirit is to 'perfect' the sons. The fiery trials of life have been designed to purge and purify the lives of the believers.

> **Hebrews 5:7** *"Who in the days of his flesh, when he had offered up prayers and supplications with strong crying and tears unto him that was able to save him from death and was heard in that he feared;*

> **(vs. 8)** *"Though He was a Son, yet taught him obedience by the things which he suffered;*

> **(vs. 9)** *"And being made prefect, He became the author of eternal salvation unto all them that obey Him;"*

The writer of Hebrews expresses that even the son Jesus, while He walked and lived in the earth experienced the maturation process. Jesus cried unto the heavenly Father with petitions and requests when he experienced anguish of the flesh.

Even though Jesus was the prototype, He coordinated the new lineage of kingdom sons. He learnt obedience through the things He suffered. Jesus was matured in His natural body to always walk in the perfect will of the Father. Jesus expressed that His only will and desire was to complete the intents of the Father who sent Him. His passions and motivations was to deny His earthly body the lustful desires of greed, bitterness, anger, sexual perversion and sin. He surrendered to the Holy Spirits navigation.

Jesus was obedient to the leading and carrying away of the Holy Spirit. He was in complete submission and surrender to the purposes of the Holy Spirit. He was in complete submission and surrender to the purposes of the Holy Spirit in His life. Hence, He became the model son and qualified to be the eternal perfect retribution for humanity's broken fellowship with the Father.

Hebrews 5:9 *"And being made perfect He became the author of eternal salvation unto all them that obey Him..."*

Jesus was made perfect as discussed and matured in the flesh. He is Lord and God but dwelt in bodily form. He had to subject it to the Holy Spirit's rulership. Through maturation and subjection, Jesus qualified to be the ultimate sacrifice for man's salvaging. Praise Jesus!

James writes about the acceptance of the navigation of the Holy Spirit in:

James 1:2-4 *"My brethren count it all joy when ye fall into divers temptations;* **(vs. 3)**

213

"Knowing this, that the trying of your faith worketh patience. **(vs. 4)**

"But let patience have her perfect work, that ye may be perfect and entire, working nothing."

(vs. 12) *"Blessed is the man that endureth temp-tation: for when he is tried, he shall receive the crown of life, which the Lord hath promise to them that love Him."*

Sons are to rejoice when they encounter temptations while walking under the full subjection of the Holy Spirit. They are not to rejoice for suffering as evil doers or busy bodies in other people's affairs.

The Sons of the Holy Spirit is to view trials as the maturing process used by the Father to purify the sons. The diversity of troubles in life are to be celebrated by the obedient son. Troubles are as the channels by which the Holy Spirit's removes the dross of sins. It is the Spirit way to expand the faith of the son in the Father. The Spirit is also leading sons into a new view of the glorious nature and character of the Heavenly Father.

The Spirit of God is producing trust in the life of sons. After the correction process patience of the sons is brought to maturity. The sons now become matured, whole and complete in the purposes of the heavenly Father.

The Sons will lack any benefit spiritually. They can now believe the Father, move swiftly and yet wait patiently until He fulfills every promise. During trials, sons now inspect their lives and begin to confess buried sin lifestyles. The sea of trials causes the sons to release any seed of the sinful nature and cry out for the transfusion of the blood of Jesus into their lives and DNA. James continues and says, *"Blessed is the man that endureth temptation."* It is important not to yield to the temptations and miss the perfecting process of the Holy Spirit. The subjected sons will receive the symbol of Sonship of royalty, which is a crown.

Sons can now walk with the nature of **royalty, kingly authority** and **influence in the earth and Spiritual realms.** The "crown of life" is the gift restored to the sons by Jesus Christ.

The crown symbolizes authority, wealth, government, rulership, royalty and kingdom. Hence, Jesus now is re-establishing the original plan of the Father to establish His heavenly Kingdom in the earth. Jesus now uses His sacrifice of death, the gift of the Holy Spirit and trials of life to re-store obedient kingdom sons in the earth. The King's Sons are now positioned with a renewed identity to their true nature essence and pose in the co-ownership of the Father's Kingdom.

The crown of life not only represents the kingly call or kingly anointed but also the life of great abundance.

215

This word <u>life</u> comes from the God-like, kingly abundant life. It signifies that the sons of God now walk above the mediocrity of a life outside of identity and royalty. No longer will the sons be subjected to poverty, lack diseases and the lust of the flesh. Through Jesus, sons will no longer be under the dominion and government of pleasing the sensual desires but now has the potential to walk in the life of Christ Jesus. Sons can now walk in the pre-fallen Adamic life. The constant dwelling of the Holy Spirit unlocks the rivers of wisdom, power, creativity, council and direct on link to the Father. Sons can now rule like Adam and the second Adam Jesus Christ. The anointing or enablement of the Holy Spirit can now flow from the heart and throne of the Father to the Holy Spirit in mankind.

The Father can breathe life, strength and healing from His throne through the Holy Spirit into the lives of the obedient Sons. He can stream the flow of His love and life into the brokenness of man's existence. His agape, 'unconditional love' can now saturate the lives of all His children. His '<u>shalom</u>,' peace and wholeness can finally wrap around the hearts of His dearest sons in the earth. He can now restore His fellowship and intimacy with His children. He can unfold the plans He has to prosper and bless His children in the earth. He can now navigate them through the jungles of life and carefully lead His sons into safety and peace. The Father can now lead His sons to the riches and glory of this life; the hidden treasure of secret places.

He can now imprint such a powerful self - awareness and image of Godly authority into their lives that they would never be deterred. The sons that now love the Father and the son Jesus can be propelled into co-heir of the Kingdom business of the Father. Access is granted to the sons to walk in the supernatural fellowship, provision and rulership both now and in the ages to come.

The Sons can now sit in the blood meetings of the Father, Son and Holy Spirit and cooperate in the family affairs. Sons can take the assignments from the Lord and fulfill them for greater rewards, bonus and partnership in the company. The sons can be seated in the heavenly places of the executive council in the Kingdom of God Cooperation and have all resources in the earth to complete their purpose in Christ.

I Peter 1:3 *"Blessed be the God and Christ, which according to His abundant mercy hath begotten us again unto a lively hope by the resurrection of Jesus Christ from the dead,*

(vs. 4) *"To an inheritance incorruptible and undefiled, and that fadeth not away, reserved in heaven for you,"*

(vs. 5) *"Who are kept by the power of God through faith unto salvation ready to be revealed in the last time."*

(vs. 6) *"Wherein ye greatly rejoice, though now for a season, if need be ye are in heaviness through manifold temptations:"*

(vs. 7) *"That the trial of your faith, being much more precious than of gold that perisheth, though it be tried with fire, might be found unto praise and honour and glory at the appearing of Jesus Christ."*

Peter, an ambassador of the government of Jesus Kingdom expressed that the Father had birth us through Jesus Christ. The writer expresses the scripture that overwhelming mercy, favor and love motivated the Father to restore the lost Sons identity. It was through the resurrection of Jesus Christ from the dead that the atonement for the broken relationship between the Father and the son. Through one man sin entered the world in Adam and through the second man Jesus' blood atonement was made. Righteousness or right relationship of man with the Father was restored through Jesus Christ.

The family of humanity had privileged to reconcile their severed family ties with the Father and His kingdom business. The sons had rights and privileged to adoption by the Father. They also have reassurance of the inheritance of the Father. The Father made provisions through Jesus Christ for the Zoa life on earth but an incorruptible undefiled inheritance in heaven. The sons would have an inheritance conveyed unto them that was guaranteed and was not decaying in nature. The inheritance was pure perfect and established in the heavens by the Father.

Peter admonishes the sons to rejoice in the midst of calamity because it last seasonally. Sons are to celebrate that the Holy Spirit's leading propels them to be made perfect through temptations.

Peter clarifies that the trial of the faith in the Father and His eternal plan in the lives of the sons will be made pure. It will be made precious and valuable in the lives of the sons will be more tangible and real than any other material object. It will be more costly than of the purest gold.

The sons' faith will not perish even though it is burnt with the fire of God testing flames. The faith of the son after being tried might be found unto the praise, honour and glory at the appearing of Jesus Christ.

The lives of the sons will cause the restoration purpose a defilement of Christ be praised by all creation. The Sons by will express the image of Jesus Christ. Praise God!

I Peter 1:14 *"As obedient children, not fashioning yourselves according to the former lust in your ignorance:*

(vs. 15) *"But as He which hath called you is Holy, be ye Holy in all manner of conversation;*

(vs. 16) *"Because it is written, be ye holy; for I AM holy.*

(vs. 17) *"And if ye call on the Father, who without respect of persons judgeth according to every man's work, pass the time of your sojourning here in fear:*

(vs. 18) *"Forasmuch as ye know that ye were not redeemed with corruptible things, as silver and gold, from your vain conversation received by tradition from your fathers;*

(vs. 19) *"But with the precious blood of Christ, as of a lamb without blemish and without spot…"*

II Corinthians 6:16 *"And what agreement hath the temple of God with idols? For ye are the temple of the living God; as God hath said, I will dwell in them, and walk in them; and I will be their God* *and they shall be my people."* **(vs. 18)** *"And will be my sons and daughters, saith the Lord Almighty."*

Psalm 2:7 *"I will declare the decree: the LORD hath said unto me, Thou art my Son; this day have I begotten thee"*

(vs. 8) *"Ask of me, and I shall give thee the heathen for thine inheritance, and the uttermost parts of the earth for thy possession."*

The writer in the book of Corinthians articulates the summary of the purposes of the covenantal relationship between the Father and the son. He questions the ungodly relationship of sons with idolatry. He describes the human body as the temple of God. The analogy of the temple is the representative of the human inner being as the dwelling place the promise of the Holy Spirit.

The heavenly Father mapped the awesome restoration plan to connect the covenantal relationship of sons to the Father. He orchestrated the fitting of the Holy Spirit into the hearts of the sons. The Father stated that He would dwell and walk with the sons. The living Father supernaturally arranged the intertwining of His presence in the hearts of all his sons.

He committed His presence to merging with the spirits of man to live intimately forever. The Father said that He would be their God; the sovereign ruler and king of all His sons. As king, He would ensure all protection of His children. The benefits of provision love and nurturing would flow from the heart of the father to His sons. He would be the source of all His sons needed in the earth and heavens to be prosperous. The Father yearned to be the God and substance for His sons; He desired that they would submit to being His offspring.

The Father wants a people, set apart unto His purposes, will and nature in the earth. The vision is the original heart of the Father when He created man in His image and likeness in the book of Genesis.

Mankind fell to rebellion through Adam the father of all humanity. The vision of the heavenly Father was distorted and now man lost the capacity to reproduce offspring in the nature of the Holy Father. Hence, through the life of the son Jesus, the Father made provisions to call a people unto Him. The Father calls forth in the earth through the Holy Spirit lost sons. He desires a nation of sons who functions as kings and priest in the earth.

Revelations 1:5 *"And from the Jesus Christ, who is the faithful witness, and the first begotten of the dead and the prince of the* *kings of the earth. Unto Him that loved us and washed us, from our sins in His own blood,*

(vs. 6) *"And hath made us Kings and Priest unto God and His Father; to Him be glory and dominion forever and ever. AMEN."*

Jesus Christ, the second Adam and the first birthed from the dead into eternal life is the prince of the new lineage of sons God. The sons were royalty, kingly in position and nature as sons of God the Father. The blood of Jesus cleansed humanity of the old sinful nature and has given access to sonship.

Jesus was made in functions as kingly and priestly. The kingly nature of the sons expresses the essence of the Father as king, Lord and sovereign maker of all that exist. The anointing or enablement of the king given to the son being allows them to rule and reign. A king has ownership over a territory, a region; possess great resources and rules over a domain. The king has great influence and is the sovereign leader over His domain. Jesus has given and restored this character to Sons who are obedient to His Spirit.

These obedient Sons would not rule from their intellect or emotions only but will rule from the advice and nature of the righteous Father. The sons will rule over their families, communities, nation and nations over the earth in co-administration with the Heavenly Father.

Sons would be managers over the earth and it's resource to the king's mandate. This partnership would be continued through an intimate covenantal relationship. Jesus has made the sons of the earth; kings and priests unto the Father who is our God.

The priestly nature of the Sons of God has the function of worship, prayer, fellowship with the Father, and relationship to other sons in the earth. The *Lexical Aids* to the New Testament describes the term priest as **'Hiereus'** (Greek) is a sacred person, serving at God's altar but not implying that He also is HOLY.

The priests of God were concerned in the nation of Israel with petitioning the Father on behalf of the people. They were responsible for the burning of incense and preparing the customs of the temple dedicated to Jehovah God. The priestly function also included the arranging of praises, musical songs and worship unto the Heavenly Father. The Father loves worship and grants access to His throne room through the blood of Jesus and thanksgiving. In that era, prior to the restoration of sons as **Kings** and **Priests**. The function of priest was confined to the tribes of Levi and Aaron.

The other citizens of the kingdom of Israel were solely subjects to limited access to the fellowship and partnership in the worship and petitioning of sons. Sons were isolated from the duties of the spiritual ordinances in their confes-sions of sins to a high priest who went into the Holy pres-ence of the Father on behalf of the people. Jesus restored the functions of the sons as recorded in **1 Peter 2 as** "stones are built up a spiritual house, a holy priesthood, to offer up spiri-tual sacrifices, acceptable to God by Jesus Christ."

> **I Peter 2 (vs. 9)** *"But ye are a chosen generation a royal priesthood, a holy nation, a peculiar people; that ye should shew forth the praises of Him who hath called you out of darkness into His marvelous light:*
>
> **(vs. 10)** *"Which in time past were not a people but are now the people of God: which had not obtained mercy, but now have obtained mercy?"*

Peter represents that the sons are a spiritual house, a holy priesthood. The priesthood has now been extended through Jesus to the obedient sons. They are consecrated, holy and set apart unto services of the King. Sons will offer spiritual sacrifices unto the Father by Jesus Christ.

The sons are now a chosen generation, a selected group of people to impact the era that they live in through kingdom principles. A royal priesthood is the kingly priest rising up by Jesus in the earth. They are the sons who function in royal order and priestly love to fellow humans.

Vines Complete Exposition Dictionary states that priest hood as priests' office. The Greek is **'hierateuma'** (2406) denotes priesthood, *"a body of priest consisting of all believers, the whole church."* The royal priesthood reveals the royal dignity of manifesting the Lord's excellence and glory. The priesthood exemplifies the authoritative office, quality, level and role in ministry of a priest.

The Father envisions a nation of sons who were both kingly and priestly. He desired a nation of sons who are royal priest under the prince Jesus. They would administer the Father's rule under the Holy Spirit. The Father as king assigns Jesus as prince over the kings in the earth, the sons. With this chain of command the Father can flow His eternal plans and anointing through His Son and sons. The sons would be peculiar, unique people in the earth among the lost sons and chaos of the present age.

The Sons of the kingdom are called in the earth to influence and express the glory of Jesus. They are to go into the arenas of business, government, politics, medicine and the nations of the earth. They are to show and exude the life essence of Jesus Christ.

Through their lives, the sons will show the praises of the righteous king. The power of sonship is demonstrated in schools, colleges, and the marketplaces. One's colleagues should be convinced of the higher life of a son. In the midst of economic turmoil, fears of terrorist attacks and financial dilemma, sons will walk in peace. Persons around will identify that these individuals are not living according to this world's standard. When sons show love and forgiveness, even though a supervisor tries to fire them; many will see the love of the Father in there unmentioned love to their enemies.

"God's plan is for His sons and daughters to inherit the earth through Jesus Christ. He set spiritual father in the body to bring them into maturity and fullness of destiny" according to '*The Turning Point*' by Apostle Emmanuella Mc Hatton.

The state of waste and want is in direct contrast to the command God gave His son in Genesis to, "multiply, replenish the earth…" The multiplication and replenishing can only come from the spiritual DNA of Christ being received and given in the life exchange of relationships. Springing from the Father Christ is the word, and the word is the seed. Sonship is seen in those who have the ability to multiply and bring increase from heaven into the earth because they have allowed themselves to be fathered. They understand and have received the grace of God. Their identity has been established purely in Christ. They draw their purpose and every reason for their existence from their Father in heaven. Many sons believe that anointing, ministry or mantles is their only inheritance from their spiritual fathers. But the essence of the inheritance was the spiritual <u>transfer</u> of <u>authority</u> and <u>honour</u> as a son to sit and rule or govern with and just like his Father.

We are not alone in our spiritual identity, but we are set in the family of God. The sons are co-heirs and rule with the son of God and share in everything that He has received from the Father. They are owners like their Father in the kingdom of heaven, entrusted with spiritual government over the earth.

The sons of God are *"sons of the light and walk in the power of the light."* When sons function in full kingdom authority from the place of relationship with the Father, many deep and profound changes will take place in nations and in creation. The earth moans and groans with pains for the revelation of the sons of God.

The Sons of God will function in the dominion of the kingdom of their Father. Ruling in true authority comes from their relationship with Him. They will bring all things into order through peace, safety, health, prosperity, and covenant relationship. The needs of the earth and its people will be met in overflowing provision. It is a covenant establish through the work Christ finished on the cross. Under His covenant, things are completed, made safe and whole restored to the Father. By the sons receiving impartation through obeying the Father and their spiritual fathers they receive tremendous blessings. Their own cycle of greed and covetousness will be broken, and they now move from to a place of fullness and completion.

It is then that the Father God sets and ordains them with authority to be fathers to the nations. The sons whom the Father pour into the nations will rise up whole nations of sons into divine destiny and relationship.

Sons of God are also the manifestation of the government of His kingdom, and of His Christ. It is upon the first born son's shoulders that the government of the kingdom of God rest. True sonship results in the sons of God ruling the earth.

> *II* **Corinthians 6:16** *"And what agreement hath the temple of God with idols? For ye are the temple of the living God; as God hath said, I will dwell in them, and walk in them; and I will be their God, and they shall be my people."*

> **(vs. 18)** *"And will be a Father unto you, and ye shall be my sons and daughters, saith the Lord Almighty."*

The vision of the Father was to establish a lineage of Sons who would dwell in His presence and fellowship with the Holy Spirit in that earth. The invitation has been re-issued after the death of the first begotten son Jesus Christ. However, the original idea of sons was implemented in the creation of Adam in the garden.

The created son, Adam, in the pre-fallen stated presented the union and communication of man with the heavenly Father. Adam had an unclogged, flow of God's river of love, blessing, favour and ability in his life.

Jesus came to restore this intimacy of the heavenly Father with His disobedient and rebellious children. Jesus came with a restorative and redemptive plan to reunite the family of God.

> **John 1:11-12** *"He came unto His own, and His own received Him not, But as many as received Him, to them gave He the power to become the sons of God, even to them that believe in His name."*

The Apostle John declares that Jesus, the Son of God, fashioned His spirit into a body and presented Himself to the nation of Israel. Jesus after 30 years of living in the nation of Israel announced His ministry, purpose and identity as the king of a heavenly kingdom. He declared His God-like char-acter, nature and relationship to the Jewish people. He truth- fully exposed His identity as being God the Father walking in the flesh of a human body.

Sadly, He was rejected and criticized as being solely the son of Mary and Joseph and not a king. "How could this Jesus whom we saw grow up in our community be the messiah?" The Jews must have thought.

However, to those that believed on His claims to God and kingship; He gave power to become sons. The book of Genesis classically outlines the creation of Adam and Eve, the parents of humanity. Adam was made in the image and likeness of God and Eve was sculptured out of Adam. Hence all humanity that was produced by His union throughout the ages represents the creation and children of God.

> **Genesis 1:26** *"And God said, Let us make man in our image and after our likeness: and let them have dominion over the fish of the sea, over the fowl of the air, and over the cattle and over all the earth, and over every creeping thing that creepeth upon the earth."*

> **(vs. 27)** *"So God created man in his own image, in the image of God created he him; male and female created He them."*

Mankind represented the seed of God the image and likeness of the Father that created them. Man, generically, was not made from the elements of the earth, sea and sky, as the case with the animals.

Contrary, man was made from the Father and He breathed His Spirit into the body of the dirt, Man then became a living thinking, God-like being who function with a body.

> **Genesis 2:7** *"And the LORD God formed man of the dust of the ground, and breathed into nostrils the breath of life; and man became a living soul."*

However, the state of the fall of man destroyed the uncontaminated flow of the Father's nature, love and spirit into the essence of man's spirit. Mankind throughout the ages rarely resembled the awesome, glorious, righteous character of the heavenly father. Hence Jesus was sent to restore the fallen state of God – character of man from the life of death, destruction and broken identity. Jesus came not to force a request of humanity to receive that He was the one who would connect the Father to man, but gave a choice. To those that received Him, to them gave He power to become the sons of God.

Therefore Jesus has the executive power not just dele-gated authority to usher children into fully mature sons. He has the liberty and authority in all of creation and heavenly realms to give mankind the ability to walk as the representative of the Kingdom of God in the earth. Jesus had all power and rights to give mankind the delegate authority to conduct the operation of the Father's business in the earth.

He also has the rights to perfect the lives of all His sons until they reflect the brilliance of His nature and glory. Jesus has the executive position and power to foster the fellowship of humanity with the majesty of the Father who is King of the Universe. Hallelujah!

The second concept that is vital to the understanding of the sonship is the words "…to them gave He power to become the sons of God."

The words 'to become' highlight an interesting position of reference to walk into sonship. This description is described in the *Lexical Aids* to the New Testament **as Ginomai (1096) or gignomai, to become, from geino or geno`- to form.** It expresses to be made of formed.

🖋 To be made or created from nothing.

🖋 To be filled or accomplished.

Hence, Jesus has legal rights to give all that accept His assignment to legal authority of Sonship. Walking in the life of a son of God in the earth is not just an instant act. The scripture here expressed a concept of an individual having the delegate authority from Jesus to be crafted into the image of God. Scripture admonishes the believer to be formed into the image of Christ.

Romans 6:1 *"What shall we say then? Shall we continue in sin, that grace may abound?*

(vs. 2) *"God forbid. How shall we that are dead to sin, live any longer there in?*

(vs. 3) *"Know ye not, that so many of us were baptized into Jesus Christ were baptized into His death?*

(vs. 4) *"Therefore we are buried with Him by baptism into death: that like as Christ was raised up from the dead by the glory of the Father, even so we also should walk in heavens of life."*

(vs. 6) *"Knowing this, that our old man is cruci-fied with Him, that the body of sin might be destroyed, that henceforth we should not serve sin.*

(vs. 11) *Likewise reckon ye also yourselves to be dead indeed unto sin, but alive unto God through Jesus Christ our Lord.*

(vs. 12) *"Let not sin therefore reign in your mortal body, that ye should obey it in the lust thereof.*

(vs. 13) *"Neither yield ye your members as instruments of unrighteousness unto sin: but yield yourselves unto God, as those that are alive from the dead, and your members as instruments of righteousness unto God.*

(vs. 14) *"For sin shall not have dominion over you: for ye are not under the law, but under grace.*

(vs. 16) *"Know ye not, that to whom ye yield your-selves servants to obey, his servants ye are to whom ye obey; whether of sin unto death, or of obedience unto righteousness?*

(vs. 22) *"But now being made free from sin, and become servants to God, ye have your fruit unto holi-ness, and the end everlasting life."*

Paul the Apostle of Jesus admonishes the believers at Rome to die to the sinful nature and live to the life of Christ. This scripture is consistent with becoming sons, Jesus offers to humanity. Paul states that the believers are baptized into Christ death.

The old nature of the lost sons and immature sons is crucified and dead to sin. He admonishes the sons to become mature sons by daily relinquishing the nature of sinful lifestyles.

The plea to the children is life unto Jesus Christ, the walk of Godlikeness. Sin is not encouraged to have dominion authority over the sons of God. It should not dictate the decisions and focus of sons. Sin should be daily mortified in the nature of the Sons.

The members of the son's bodies must be used as vehicles for the righteous nature of the Father; thus allowing the flow of God's love and righteousness to produce a lifestyle of the Kingdom of Christ.

Sons are to be the extension of the Father to the lost children in their earth. They are to touch other humans through the love and righteousness of the Father. These are the keys to becoming the sons of God. Children born to God through Jesus Christ mature to sons through the separation of sin and evil; and gravitating to the righteous life-nature of the Heavenly Father.

Jesus expresses the born-again experience of lost sons into children and maturity in sons of God.

> **John 3:3** *"Jesus answered and said unto him, verily, verily I say unto thee, except a man be born again, he cannot see the Kingdom of God.*

(vs. 4) *Nicodemus saith unto him, how can a man be born when he is old? Can he enter the second time into his mother's womb, and be born?*

(vs. 5) *"Jesus answered, Verily, verily, I say unto thee, except a man is born of water and of the Spirit, he cannot enter in the kingdom of God."*

A young ruler Nicodemus questions the King about His kingdom in the earth. Nicodemus had lived under laws and tutors as a Pharisee but once converse with King Jesus who spoke with authority. Jesus began to introduce the restorative plan of humanity to sonship. He details that humanity must now be birth again into the original DNA of God. Mankind must now enter into childhood through Jesus Christ and mature into sons through the righteous life of the sons.

Jesus declares that regardless of a man's chronological age He must be born again to see the kingdom of God. The kingdom of God is the rule and reign of God over a terri-tory operating under the **laws, precepts and decrees of the king.** Unless man is dead to sin and be born again through the name and blood of Jesus; they cannot even glimpse the lifestyle of the kingdom nor relationship with the King.

Sons cannot walk in maturity and live in the realm of the Kingdom living without intimate communication with the king. The king wants the kingdom to be seen by His sons and experience by His obedient sons. The king wants to smear His nature on the sons through continuous interaction. He wants the fragrance of His glory to rest upon His sons. He yearns for His sweet Spirit presence to aromatize the life of His sons. Through the Kings communion with His sons He desires to give to them the kingdom.

John 3:6 *"That which is born of the flesh; and that which is born of the spirit is spirit."*

The Father desires His sons not to be birth out of fleshly lust and sinful nature that govern their lives. He desires to birth Spiritual sons with the genetics of the heavenly Father through the blood can be visualized as a transfusion of an individual; blood is drawn from one arm and the blood of Jesus is spiritually transfused into the other arm of the Sons.

Ephesians 5:1 *"Be ye therefore followers of God as dear children:*

(vs. 2) *"And walk in love, as Christ also hath loved us, and hath given Himself for us an offering and a sacrifice to God for a sweet-smelling savour.*

(vs. 3) *"But fornication, and all uncleanness, or covetousness, let it not be named among you, as becometh saints;"*

(vs. 5) *"For this ye know, that no whoremonger, nor unclean person, nor covetous man, who is an idolater, hath any inheritance in the kingdom of Christ and of God.*

(vs. 6) *"Let no man deceive you with vain words: for because of these things becometh the wrath of God upon the children of disobedience."*

(vs. 7) *"Be not ye therefore partners with them."* **(vs. 8)** *"For ye were sometimes darkness, but now are ye light in the Lord: walk as children of light."*

Again, the maturation process of sons requires the Holy Spirit to partner with obedience sons to birth the life of Christ.

Philippians 2:13 *"For it is God which worketh in you both <u>to will</u> and to do of His good pleasure."*

(vs. 14) *"Do all things without murmurings and disput-ings:* **(vs. 15)** *"That ye may be blameless and harm-less the sons of God, without rebuke, in the midst of a crooked and perverse nation among whom ye shine as lights in the world;"*

Sons are to be exemplary in their character and behaviour in the family, community and marketplace. Their nature should be one of peaceable, patient and spirit-led. The brilliant life radiating in a world of wickedness, corruption and darkness will glorify the Spirit of the Father. The sons will arise in the nations of the earth and restore the order of the kingdom principles in all spheres of human interaction. **The life of the sons will shine in the uttermost, gatherings of humanly interaction, government, politics, business, medicine, law and schools.**

> **Galatians 5:16** *"This I say then walk in the Spirit, and ye shall not fulfill the lust of the flesh."*
>
> **(vs. 17)** *"For the flesh lusteth against the spirit, and the spirit against the flesh: and these are contrary the one to the other: so that ye cannot do the things that ye would.* **(vs. 18)** *"But if ye be led of the Spirit, ye are not under the law."*
>
> **(vs. 22)** *"But the fruit of the spirit is love, joy, peace, longsuffering, gentleness, goodness, faith,*
>
> **(vs. 23)** *Meekness, temperance: against such there is no law.*

(vs. 24) *"And they that are Christ's have cruci-fied the flesh with the affections and lusts."*

(vs. 25) *"It we live* **John 1:12** *"...even to them that believe on His name:"*

(vs. 13) *"Which were born, not of blood, nor of the will of the flesh, nor of the will of man but of God?"*

Sons will be birthed through the affirmation in the name of Jesus. The 'name' generally specifies the character of an individual. Name carries with it the authority of that individual the credibility of the life of the person.

The name of Jesus carries tremendous authority in the natural and spiritual realms. *"At the name of Jesus every knee shall bow and every tongue confess that He is owner of everything."* His name also provides access to the father; it is the only name whereby mankind can be salvaged and restored to sonship. It is through the name, authority credibility and influence of Jesus that sons are born in the Spirit. The sons can be born in the will of the father Praise God!!!!

Chapter 15— End of Chapter Principles

∀ Sons have the genetic make-up of their heavenly Father to be present His character, nature and love in the earth!

∀ Sons are lead away or directed by the Holy Spirit.

∀ Jesus learnt obedience through the things He suffered.

∀ Sons should welcome challenges and life's trials as part of the maturation process.

∀ Sons are Ambassadors of the Kingdom of Jesus Christ. They are delegated envoys involved in possessing territories.

∀ Sons are dual in Kingdom function as Kingly and Priestly. The Kingly represents government and authority in the earth. Priestly represent access to the Father, worship and fellowship with the Father.

∀ **Royal Priestly hood indicates the royal dignity of showing forth the Lord's excellence.**

∀ **Sons will restore kingdom laws and values to families' workplace, government, education, cities and various until it resembles Heaven's operation.**

Chapter 16

Adopted into the
Kingly Family

!"

*Romans 8:15 "For ye have not received the spirit
of bondage again to fear; but ye have received
the Spirit of adoption whereby we cry, Abba,
Father."*

The Father's love fueled His passion to restore wayward sons back to His Kingdom through Jesus Christ. He had a magnificent plan to engraft lost immature children into the family tree of mature spirit lead sons in the earth. Within the ability of humanly nature it was impossible for mankind to attain the God-like image as sons. Mankind was smeared with the blanket of deceit from an unloving, abusive step-father Satan.

Satan had gotten perversely the rights to the authority, inheritance and the keys to the fears and destruction of man. He obtained these deeds in the garden of Eden, when man disobeyed His true father and obeyed a false father. For thousands of years, mankind lived as lost children wondering in the earth deprived of identity; controlled by death and fear.

Romans 5:17 *"For if by one man's offense death reigned by one; much more they which receive abun-dance of grace and of the gift of righteousness shall reign in life by one, Jesus Christ.)"*

(vs. 18) *"Therefore as by the offense of one judgment came upon all men to condemnation; even so by the righteousness of one the free gift came upon all men unto justification of life."*

(vs. 19) *"For as by one man's disobedience many were made sinners so by the obedience of one shall many be made righteous."*

(vs. 21) *"That as sin hath reigned unto death even so might grace reign through righteousness unto eternal life by Jesus Christ our Lord."*

Hebrews 2:14-17 *"Forasmuch then as the children are partakers of flesh and blood, He also Himself likewise took part of the same; that through death He might destroy him that had the power of death, that is, the devil:*

(vs. 15) *"And deliver them who through fear of death were their entire lifetime subject to bondage."* **(vs. 16)** *"For verily he took not on him the nature*

of angles; but he took on him the seed of Abraham. **(vs. 17)** *"Wherefore in all things it behoved him to be made like unto his brethren, that he might be made a merciful and faithful high priest in things pertaining to God, to make reconciliation for the sins of the people."*

Jesus Christ the eldest son came into the earth in the nature of humanity to be an intercessor between the Father and the sons in the earth. An intercessor is described as one who stands between individuals and makes request and partitioning on behalf of another. Jesus is the gap-connector, the bridge, between the Father and humanity. He came to destroy, set free and deliver the sons in the earth entangled by the fear of death.

The spirit of fear choked life, evoking death and daily circumstances. The destructive flames of fear were fanned by Satan, the false father. He does not operate by love and liberty but by fear and bondage. God has not given His sons a spirit of fear but of love, power and a sound mind.

Paul writes in **Romans 8:15** that the sons of God have not accepted the spirit of fear that places them in bondage. Fear has no more power over sons; for living a victorious life. No longer will sons feel abandoned and detached from the loving protection of their God.

Think about our circumstances, imagine a child disobeying their parents and skipping school. The fear that overwhelms that child if caught in the mall by his father. The child is aware of his disobedience and understands that he was outside of the mercy of his father. However, when he is caught by his father, he cautiously corrects him but showed him mercy and forgiveness. This is similar to the fear of humanity to its loving father. The children in the earth were disobedient and trespassed the boundaries of the laws of the Father.

They had no other disposition than to be afraid that the goodness, favour and mercy of their Father were not warranted. Humanity, until the ministry of Jesus was so detached from the concept of relationship with the Heavenly Father that they did not call Him Abba. The Heavenly Father was viewed as a mystical dreary old faced, long beard God who sat on a gigantic golden throne. He was viewed as of one who would quickly strike down any person in His way for pleasure and laughed with thunderously echoes in the earth. Mankind was in slavery to fear of even approaching the Father; His Holy name was not even mention or written as *Yahweh* or *Jehovah*. Yet symbols were used to refer to Him and only a selected group of high priests were allowed to enter His presence once a year to represent the people in Israel.

Jesus erected a new order of referring to the most Holy creator and God as father (Abba); it was an insult to the religious of his times. His claims of intimate relationship with Jehovah God were absurd and blasphemous they thought. How dare Jesus make Himself equal and personal with this majestic creator?

Jesus revolutionized the concept of sonship in His generation and the ages that proceeded. He re-established the foundation of family intimacy and identity of sons with their true source the father. Jesus introduced the plan to engraft the descendants of Adam back into the family tree of heaven. His plans, missions and assignments were to re-attached sons to their source through the Holy Spirit.

"...But ye have received the spirit of adoption, whereby we cry, Abba, Father."

Paul, the ambassador of the Kingdom writes that the sons will not be restricted by the deceptive fears of Satan but will receive the liberty by the Holy Spirit. Sons shall receive the spirit of Jesus Christ. It is the Holy Spirit or the Parakletos, who would instruct, advocate, advise, direct and lead the children into the maturity as Sons.

> **John 14:15** *"If ye love me, keep my commandment."* **(vs. 16)** *"And I will pray the Father, and He shall give you another Comforter, that He may abide with you forever;"*

> **(vs. 26)** *"But the Comforter which is the Holy Ghost, whom the Father will send in my name, He shall teach you all things, and bring to your remem-brance whatsoever I have said unto you."*

Jesus in the above scriptures declares that He would send the Comforter on the disciples in Jerusalem 2,000 years ago but also on the saints "Sons of God" throughout the ages. The Holy Spirit will abide with the obedient sons forever. His assignment was activated by the sacrifice and name of Jesus. The Father sent Him on the creditial influence and power of the name of Jesus. *"Every knee shall bow and tongue must confess in heaven and earth that Jesus is Lord."* Jesus through His life as a Son walked sinless and righteous. He has secured a name above every other name in existence. His name signifies life, power, influence and authorized right to rule everything. At the name of Jesus, demons flee, disease dry up, circumstances change and lost children can become kingdom sons of power. Hallelujah!!

The Father sends the Holy Spirit to adopt the immature isolated children of God. The Holy Spirit's assignment among many others is to begin the refining process of remodeling the nature and DNA of humanity. He must train the immature children in walking like King's kids. The Holy Spirit has to adopt children from the foster home of the flesh and bring them into the righteousness of the palace. **He has to take those who all through their lives have experience brokenness, rejection, abuse, destruction and emptiness into victorious majestic royal sons**.

> **John 16:7** *"Nevertheless I tell you the truth: it is expedient for you that I go away: for if I go not away the Comforter will not come unto you; but if I depart, I will send Him unto you."*
>
> **(vs. 8)** *"And when He is come, He will reprove the world of sin, and of righteousness, and of judgment:*

(vs. 9) *"Of sin, because they believe not on me;* **(vs. 10)** *"Of righteousness, because I go to my*
Father, and ye see me more;

(vs. 11) *"Of judgment, because the prince of the world is judged."*

(vs. 13) *"How be it, when He, the Spirit of truth is come, He will guide you into all truth; for He shall not speak of Himself; but whatsoever He shall hear, that shall He speak: and He will shew you things to come."*

(vs. 14) *"He shall glorify me: for He shall receive of mine, and shall shew it unto you."*

(vs. 15) *"All things that the Father hath are mine: therefore said I, that He shall take of mine, and shall shew it unto you."*

Jesus in the above scriptures outlines the work of the person of the Holy Spirit. He is the King's tutor perfecting the thoughts, intents and character of the sons of God. Praise God! Paul defines this magnificent transfer of sons from, ignorance into revelation of their identity. The immaturity children are translated from the kingdom of light through Jesus Christ. The metamorphosis of sons of Satan and the Holy Spirit is described in **Romans 8**.

The term adoption is key to the concept of the redemp-tive plan of children to sons. Adoption comes from the Greek word *'Huiothesisa'* (5206) according to the *Lexical Aids* to the New Testament. It stems from two words, *'Huios'* (5207), son, and *tithemi* (5087), to place.

'Huios'- signifies the relationship of offspring to parent. It refers to those who show maturity acting as sons. It describes the dignity of one's relationship and representa-tion of God's character and nature.

'Tithemi' means to appoint, set, reserve, assign, and constitute. The concept in the term adoption is receiving another unto the relationship of a child of someone. A person is appointed as a son; now legal guardian rights are given to the parents.

The Father adopts into the Covenant of Abraham as sons

> **Galatians 3:7** *"Know ye therefore that they which are of faith the same are the children of Abraham."* **(vs. 23)** *"But before faith came we were kept under the law shut up unto the faith which should afterwards be revealed."*

(vs. 24) *"Wherefore the law was our school-master to bring us unto Christ, that we might be justified by faith.*

(vs. 25) *"But after that faith is come we are no longer under a schoolmaster.*

(vs. 26) *"For ye are all the children of God by faith in Christ Jesus."*

(vs. 27) *"For as many of you as have been baptized into Christ have put on Christ."*

(vs. 28) *"There is neither Jew nor Greek, there neither bond or free, there is neither male nor female: for ye are all one in Jesus Christ:*

(vs. 29) *"And if ye be Christ's, then are ye Abraham's seed, and heirs according to the promise."*

Paul establishes that the people, who receive the life of Jesus, can now be engrafted into the lineage of Abraham by faith. Immature children in eras prior to Jesus' restoration plan were adoption states the place and condition of son given to one to whom it does not naturally belong.

Vines Complete Expository Dictionary states, "In **Romans 8:15**, believers are said to have received

253

"the spirit of adoption," that is, the Holy Spirit who, given as the first fruit of all that is to be theirs, produces in them the realization of sonship and the attitude belonging to sons.

Sonship bestowed in distinction from a relationship consequence merely upon birth. God does not "adopt" believers as children; they are begotten as such by His Holy Spirit through faith. "Adoption" is a term involving the dignity of the relationship of believers as a son. The Father has taken the responsibility of protecting, providing and caring for His sons. He has assumed the role, like a natural father of discipline, nurturing, encouraging in distressing times and forming His image in His Sons.

Daddy has taken the role to nurture His sons into their destinies. He desires to be trusted as the sole source of His son's existence. He wants to fuel the fulfillment of the destinies of His sons.

The Kingdom of God is built by working with the Spirit of God to perform signs, miracles and wonders for the glory of the Father. God's rule and order of the heavenly kingdom and on earth will be seen in this era of humanity. In heaven there is order, structure, peace, glory, and worship of God. The Supreme rulership of the Father will be established in the earth as it functions in Heaven. Hallelujah!!!!

Genetics of a Son

Philippians 2:15 *"That ye may be blameless and harmless the sons of God, without rebuke in the midst of a crooked and perverse nation, among whom ye shine as lights in the world."*

- Son is a seed of the Father (nature).
- Son is the continuation of the species.
- Sons have a heart for the affairs of the Father.
- Sons resemble the Father (spiritually).
- Sons receive self-awareness from the Father (identity).
- Sons conduct business on behalf of the Father.
- Sons have authorization of the Father in the earth.
- Sons have the inheritance of the Father.
- Sons show the wealth and the glory.
- Sons know the heart and will of the Father.
- The Father corrects sons.
- Sons are committed to being taken care of by the Father.

Keys to Living a Spirit-led life includes:

✎ Accept Jesus Christ.

✎ Prayer and fasting.

✎ Mortify the Flesh.

✎ Obey the Word of God.

- Accept the Kingdom and Walk in the Kingdom.

- Worship.

- Fellowship with the Father.

  Fellowship with other Sons

End of Book Scripture

References and Principles

Ephesians 1:2 *"Grace be to you, and peace, from God our Father, and from the Lord Jesus Christ.*

(vs. 3) *"Blessed be the God and Father of our Lord Jesus Christ who hath blessed us with all spiritual blessings in heavenly places in Christ.*

(vs. 4) *"According as He hath chosen us in Him before the foundation of the world that we should be Holy and without blame before Him in Love:*

(vs. 5) *"Having predestinated us into the adoption of children by Jesus Christ to Himself, according to the good pleasure of His will."*

Ephesians 2:4 *"But God who is rich in mercy, for His great love where with He loved us,*

(vs. 5) *"Even when we were dead in sins hath quickened us together with Christ, (by grace ye are saved;)*

(vs. 6) *"And hath raised us up together, and made us sit together in heavenly places in Christ Jesus:*

(vs. 7) *"That in the ages to come He might show the exceeding riches of His grace in His kindness toward us through Christ Jesus."*

Ephesians 2:18 *"For through Him we both have access by one Spirit unto the Father"*

(vs. 19) *"Now therefore ye are no more strangers and foreigners, but fellow citizens with the saints and of the household of God;*

(vs. 20) *"And are built upon the foundation of the apos-tles and prophets, Jesus Christ Himself being the Chief cornerstone;*

(vs. 21) *"In whom all building fitly framed together growth unto a Holy temple in the Lord:*

(vs. 22) *"In whom ye also are building together for a habitation of God through the Spirit."*

Sons Are Fruitful

John 15:8 *"By this, My Father is glorified, that you bear much fruit, so you will by my disciples."*

John 15:16 *"You did not choose me, but I chose you and appointed you that you should go and bear fruit and that your fruit should remain, that <u>whatever</u> you ask the Father in My name He may give you."*

Sonship Authority - "Sons are disciplined"

Hebrews 12:5 *"... and you have forgotten that word of encouragement that addresses you as sons: My son, do not make light of the Lord's discipline, and do not lose heart when He rebukes you."*

(vs. 6) *"Because the Lord disciplines those He loves, and He punishes everyone He accepts as a son."*

(vs. 7) *"Endure hardship as discipline; God is treating you as sons. For what son are not disciplined by his father?"*

(vs. 8) *If you are not disciplined (and everyone under-goes discipline) then you are illegitimate children and not true sons.*

(vs. 9) *Moreover we have all had human fathers who disciplined us and we respected them for it. How much more should we submit to the Father of our spirits and live.*

(vs. 10) *"Our fathers disciplined us for a little while as they thought best; but God disciplines us for our good, that we may share in His holiness."*

(vs. 11) *"No discipline seems pleasant at the time, but painful. Later on however, it produces a harvest of righteous-ness and peace for those who have been trained by it."*

Hebrew 5:8 *"Though He were a son, yet learned the obedience by the things which he suffered."*

(vs. 9) *"And being made <u>perfect</u> (5048), He became the authority of eternally salvation unto all them that obey Him"*

<u>Son and Heirs of Christ"</u>

Galatians 3:7 *"Therefore know that only those who are of faith are sons of Abraham."*

Galatians 3:26-29 *"For you are all sons of God through faith in Christ Jesus"*

(vs. 27) *"For as many of you as were baptized into Christ have put on Christ."*

(vs. 28) *"There is neither Jew nor Greek there is neither slave nor free there is neither male nor female; for you are all in Christ Jesus.*

(vs. 29) *"And if you are Christ's, then you are Abraham's seed, and heirs according to the promise*

Galatians 4:1 *"Now I say that the heir as long as he is a child, does not differ at all from a slave, though the master of all,*

(vs. 2) *"But is under guardians and stewards until the time appointed by the Father."*

(vs. 3) *"Even so we, when we were children, were in bondage under the elements of the world.*

(vs. 4) *But when the fullness of the time has come, God sent forth His Son, born of a woman, born under the Law,*

(vs. 5) *"To redeem those who were under the law, that we might receive the adoptions as sons."*

(vs. 6) *"And because you are sons, God has sent forth the Spirit of His Son into your hearts, crying out, Abba Father!"*

(vs. 7) *"Therefore you are no longer a slave but a son, and if a son, then an heir of God through Christ."*

Sonship through the Spirit

Romans 8:12 -21

"Therefore brethren we are debtors, not to the flesh, to live according to the flesh."

(vs. 13) *"For if you live according to the flesh you die, but if by the spirit you put to death the deeds of the body, you will live."*

(vs. 14) *"For as many as are led by the Spirit of God, these are sons of God."*

(vs. 15) *"For you did not receive the Spirit of bondage again to fear; but you receive the spirit of adoption by whom we cry out. Abba, Father."*

(vs. 16) *"The Spirit himself bears witness with our spirit that we are children of God,*

(vs. 17) *"And if the children, then heirs; heirs of God and joint heirs with Christ; if indeed we suffer with Him that we may also be glorified together."*

(vs. 18) *"For I consider that the sufferings of this present time are not worthy to be compared with the glory which shall be revealed in us.*

(vs. 19) *"For the earnest expectation of the creation eagerly, waits for the revealing of the sons of God."*

(vs. 29) *"For whom He foreknew, He also predestined to be conformed to the image of His Son, that He might be the firstborn among many brethren."*

(vs. 30) *"Moreover whom He predestined, these He also called; whom He called these He also justified; and whom He justified, these He also glorified."*

John 16:14 *"He will glorify me, for He will take of what is mine and declare it to you."* **John 16:15** *"All things that the Father has are mine. Therefore, I said that He will take of mine and declare it to you."*

End of Book Principles and Concepts

!"

Maturity or perfection is a continuous process, as Christ is constantly developed in us. Sons should be free from the Spirit or nature to compete with other sons of God.

Each trajectory course is designed by the Holy Spirit and is different for each son. There may be overlapping of purpose and strategic connection the Holy Spirit may orchestrate during various seasons but ultimately He is in charge.

Church ministries according to Ephesians 4 must equip sons:

1.) In Perfection the saints to go into the marketplaces to minister. Perform works of Ministry
2.) Edify the Sons.

3.) Unify the Sons.

4.) Build the knowledge of Jesus Christ in Sons.

5.) Bring the Sons into wholeness.

6.) Develop the Sons into the stature of Christ (His nature, character, essence and likeness).

Church leaders must assist in the maturation process of Sons to mirror Christ.

Sons are to be able to hear clearly and concisely the voice of the Father for their every moments need. The accu-racy of the voice of the Father will also direct Sons into their specific assignment in Kingdom Function.

> **Philippians 2:15** *"That ye may be blameless and harmless, the sons of God, without rebuke, in the midst of a crooked and perverse nation, among whom ye shine as lights in the world."*

The lives of Sons should be blameless in speech and character in the earth, the glory of the Father must shine brilliantly through the lives of the Sons.

Power of the sons in Christ in the Earth

∀ Sons are joint heirs to Jesus' inheritance.

∀ Inheritance is delegated to faithful Sons.

∀ Power of authority is granted to mature Sons.

∀ The Father desires intimate relationship with Sons.

∀ The Father has benefits for His family of Sons.

∀ Benefits include divine favour and visitation.

∀ Divine protection is provided for Sons.

∀ Rulership over the world now and worlds to come.

∀ Sons are given biding and loosing authority.

∀ Sons are able to demonstrate self government.

∀ Sons can dispatch or send Angelic Spirits to work.

∀ The ability to call things out of the spiritual realm (invisible, intangible) into the tangible visible physical realm.

∀ Sons are ambassadors of the kingdom (Representative of the most High God).

∀ Sons assist in unifying the Kingdom. (The creation and citizens).

∀ Sons are a Kingdom of Kings. Sons have royalty, honour, and influence. Sons of a Mighty King.

Sons Authority:

! Operation in the Spiritual Realm **(Matthew 16:19).**

! Heirs to the promise of Abraham **(Genesis 17:6-7).**

God shall establish Sons and make Sons' name great.

They shall be fruitful.

! As a Son you will be called brother/brethren by Jesus.

Hebrews 2:12 *"I will declare your name to my brethren, in the midst of the assembly I will sing praise to you."*

(vs. 13) *"And again: "Here am I the children whom God has given me."*

As a Son all prophetic words are yours found in the Word of God, for example: *"No weapon formed against Sons shall prosper,"* Sons are blessed, and Sons shall never be put to shame. Sons shall have sound minds.

As a Son the Spirit of God will reveal truths and mysteries of His Kingdom. **John 16:25** *"These* *things have spoken to you in figurative language; but the time is coming when I will no longer speak to you figurative language but I will tell you plain about the Father."*

🖊 As a Son. There is Divine protection. **Hebrews 2:16** *"For indeed He does not give aid to Angels, but He does give aid to the seed of Abraham." The angel of the Lord encamps around.*

Psalms 91:11 *"For He shall give His angels charge over you, to keep you in all your ways.*

(vs. 12) *"In their hands they shall bear you up, lest you dash your foot against a stone."*

Psalm 34:7 *"The angel of the LORD encamps all around those who fear Him, and delivers them.*

🖊 Sons have a future Kingdom to inherit. Scriptures include:

🖊 **Matthew 25:34**

🖊 **I Corinthians 6:2-3**

🖊 **Revelation 4:10**

🖊 **Revelation 7:14-17**

End of Book Summary:

!"

God's Plan for Sons of the Kingdom:

✂ To train, equip and develop saints to walk and mani-fest their sonship relationship and authority in the earth.

✂ Develop sons of God who demonstrate the covenant and of relationship with the heavenly Father through Jesus Christ.

✂ To train the sons of God to manifest **authority, dominion** and **power** in the natural and spiritual realms.

✂ To equip the Sons of God to function in the Kingdom lifestyles in their spirit, mind, body, finances and family.

The most significant of all is the fact that we are as believers seated in heavenly place. The sons have a spiritual mantle; an assignment of rulership in the earth.

End of Chapter Summary

!"

- ✂ Sons given power by Jesus Christ.

- ✂ Sons matured and perfected to do the work of the Father.

- ✂ Authority as sons to overcome sins, hear the voice of God.

- ✂ Sons are to teach of kingly priesthood in the earth. They must move in the power of apostolic and prophetic power.

- ✂ Sons are joint heirs with Jesus. Their inheritance in the kingdom to come and adoption as sons of God.

- ✂ The earth moans for the sons of God to be revealed.

- ✂ Sons as matured in the faith and perfected.

- Gift of being a Son of God.

- Prosperity of Obedience as a Son of God

- The Identification and acceptance of being a Son of God.

- Sons have power to bind and loosing in the spiri-tual realm.

- Sons are born of a new seed.

- Sons have lost all earthly ties and now walk in the Kingdom.

- Nations of Sons are led by the spirit of God.

- Those whose will is to do the will of the Father in heaven.

Release of power, purpose and peace in the acceptance of being a son of God.

Kingdom of Priest and Kings of the sons: Son's role include-

🖉 Kingdom Purpose

🖉 Destiny Assignment

- Apostolic Grace

- Ambassadorship

- Authority/Dominion Power

- Endowment of Spirit Gifting.

- Sons in Government, Politics, Media, Education.

- Sons of God will establish His order in the Earth.

- Rising up of Sons of God, believers led by the Spirit of God, in all areas as of other lives. Kingdom Sons leads to transform all areas of society.

Bibliography

!"

- Vines' Complete Expository.

- Strong's Concordance.

- The King James Bible.

- Sons and Sonship- A. Hancliff.

- Rediscovering the Kingdom- Dr. Myles Munroe.

- The Turning Point- Apostle Emmanuella McHatton.